Just Enough is Plenty

Samuel Alexander

JUST ENOUGH IS PLENTY: THOREAU'S ALTERNATIVE ECONOMICS

Published by the Simplicity Institute, Melbourne, 2016

www.simplicityinstitute.org

Copyright © 2016 Samuel Alexander

All rights reserved.

Cover by Andrew Doodson © 2016

ISBN-13: 978-0-9941606-4-5

Advance praise for *Just Enough is Plenty*:

'*Just Enough Is Plenty* is a superb introduction to Thoreau's life and ideas, written with clarity and style by a leading exponent of Thoreau's economics of voluntary simplicity. Samuel Alexander expertly guides the reader through the often difficult terrain of Thoreau's economic ideas, highlighting the opportunities for living simpler, freer lives. The result will help a new generation of readers understand Thoreau's essential message – and apply it to their own lives. The benefits of doing so are potentially immense.'

– Phillip Cafaro, author of *Thoreau's Living Ethics*

CONTENTS

Acknowledgements

I sometimes wonder what it would have been like to sit down with Henry David Thoreau and have a beer. I'm not actually sure whether he drank beer. Perhaps he would have suggested that we go drink from the pond instead, or wander the moonlit woods in intoxicating silence rather than sit in some noisy, dark, over-crowded bar. If he was in one of his solitary moods, he may well have asked me just to leave him alone. Nevertheless, intimidating though it would have been, I'd like to have had an opportunity to thank him for writing such beautiful, compelling, and provocative books and essays, and for being such a deep inspiration to me and so many others. I'll never have that opportunity, of course, so let me simply pay my respects now by dedicating this publication to him.

Two short segments of this booklet have been published in *Adbusters: Journal of the Mental Environment*. A revised version of the preface was published in *Adbusters* #127 (2016) and a short section of the main text was published in *Adbusters* #89 (2013). Further snippets were published in my 'Thoreau' chapter in the collection of essays *Simple Living in History: Pioneers of the Deep Future* (2014), co-edited by myself and Amanda McLeod. I am grateful for the opportunity to reprint.

I want to thank (yet again) my wonderful editor, Antoinette Wilson, for polishing the text, and my cover designer, Andrew Doodson, for always being supportive of my work. Thank you both, most of all, for your friendship.

Compost Capitalism

I was drifting through cyberspace recently, not really absorbing the words in front of me, when I came across a sentence that tripped me up, so to speak, and forced me to pay attention. That sentence read: 'The pain you feel is capitalism dying.' The writer, Joe Brewer, went on to explain that it hurts because we are inside this dying system, we are inside this unsustainable form of civilisation while it is undermining the life support system we call Earth, and to me what is perhaps most unsettling about this is that it's not yet clear what comes next; nor is it obvious that the global problems we face even have smooth, painless solutions. The hour is dark and a bright new dawn is not guaranteed.

'The pain you feel is capitalism dying.' The words left an impression on me I think because they describe that strange, existential ache that we probably have all felt at some time or another, when contemplating how we should live our lives in a world that seems so tragically off track. I am referring here to the emotional, or what one might even call the spiritual challenge of living in an age of crisis; of living in an age when the myths and stories that have shaped and grounded our cultures and even our identities have begun to break down, unsettling our sense of purpose and place in a fast-changing world.

But this crisis of meaning in our culture, if I can put it that way, presents itself to us as a heavily disguised but tantalising opportunity. One of the most promising aspects of the biological world we live in is that the cycles of nature embrace death and decay as a necessary part of rebirth – as anyone who composts knows very well – and if we understand this, then we can see that as the existing form of life deteriorates in the face of environmental limits, new ways to live will inevitably evolve, and are evolving, like green shoots peeking out of the widening concrete cracks in capitalism. And our challenge, I think, is to face this inevitable breakdown with defiant positivity and set about turning today's crises into opportunities to reinvent ourselves, our cultures, and our economies in more localised, more resilient, and more humane ways. We are, it seems, like tiny microbes inside this massive, decomposing system, being challenged to work creatively away in our own small ways, building the soil from which a diversity of new worlds can emerge. In short, I would say that we are being challenged, at this moment in history, to compost capitalism; and in the rich soil of resistance and renewal, our task, our collective task, is to seed a new Earth story.

But how, as Charles Eisenstein would say, can we create 'the more beautiful world our hearts know is possible'? When an entire civilisation is geared toward producing and consuming more and more consumer products, it can be very difficult for people to live and think differently, very difficult to embrace a life of sufficiency – even for those of us who want to. In many ways we are 'locked in' to consumer lifestyles or 'locked on' to the industrialising path, whether we like it or not, and there is no easy, silver-bullet solution to this problem. It is always difficult to swim against the tide of civilisation.

One step that can be taken, however, is to dedicate more of our attention to exploring alternative ways of living and being, and that exploration is the defining purpose of this booklet, which focuses on the life and ideas of Henry David Thoreau (1817–1862). Now a canonical figure in American literature, Thoreau is not an easy writer to read – his sentences are often very dense, thick with allusions, metaphors, and double-meaning; his ideas, challenging and provocatively expressed. For these reasons the casual reader can be easily put off, as I was when first exposed to Thoreau. But his perspectives are too important to miss, and for that reason I sat down to write this introductory text on Thoreau to provide an accessible overview of his philosophy of voluntary simplicity, in the hope that readers will then go on to his primary texts.

Although Thoreau's practical philosophy of living has critically important political implications, the central focus of this booklet is on the personal level, which was Thoreau's focus. The political and macroeconomic analyses, necessary though they are, are most coherently undertaken *after* one has determined what a flourishing and sustainable life might look like, and on that preliminary issue I contend that there is no greater or more necessary source of wisdom and inspiration than Henry David Thoreau. I hope that his ideas and example enrich your life as they have enriched mine.

All truly wise thoughts have been thought already thousands of times; but to make them truly ours, we must think them over again honestly, till they take root in our personal experience.

– Johann Wolfgang von Goethe

JUST ENOUGH IS PLENTY

THOREAU'S ALTERNATIVE ECONOMICS

The cost of a thing is the amount of what I will call life which is
required to be exchanged for it, immediately or in the long run.
– Henry David Thoreau

1. THE PATH TO WALDEN

Graduating from Harvard in 1837 was a young student named
Henry David Thoreau. This able graduate was an aspiring poet, but
his poetry, though often beautiful and inspired, was not a
commodity that sold well in the market. Indeed, it did not sell at all.
So, upon returning to his hometown of Concord, Massachusetts, the
young Thoreau was confronted by those great economic questions
all of us must face when trying to establish financial independence
in a world of scarce resources: *How best to earn a living? How
much time should I spend at it? How much do I need to live well
and to be free?*

This extended essay examines the difficult but rewarding
struggle that ensued when Thoreau set about answering those very
human questions. It begins by trying to understand the poet's 'crisis
of vocation' and then moves on to consider his not unrelated
critique of materialistic culture. This will provide the foundations
for a sustained examination of the 'alternative economics' that

Thoreau presents in his magnificent but unclassifiable manifesto, *Walden*.[1]

Although what follows is, on the surface, about this poet-philosopher named Henry Thoreau and the response he gave to the economic situation he faced, I invite readers to consider the relevance of Thoreau's life and ideas to our own day, our own lives – our own economic situations. For as Ralph Waldo Emerson said when speaking at Thoreau's graduation ceremony: 'This time, like all times, is a very good one, if we but know what to do with it.'[2] And as for knowing what to do with it, I wish to speak a word for Thoreau.

1.1. *Crisis of Vocation*

Aside from the fact that his poetry would not sell, there were certain expectations that attached to a Harvard graduate at the time, and being a poet was not one of them. In fact, there were only a few 'respectable' career paths open to Thoreau: he could have entered the ministry, which would have been the most esteemed path; he could have gone into a secular profession such as law, politics, medicine, or teaching; or he could have begun trading as a merchant. This last option was absolutely out of the question for Thoreau, who at twenty was already contemptuous of the Boston businessman and all he stood for. The first option, entering the ministry, was almost as unattractive, due to his antipathy toward institutionalised religion and his inclination toward free-thinking mysticism.[3] Practicing law held no appeal for him, nor did a political career – both were too involved with the state for this fervent individualist.[4] And medicine did not inspire. That left only teaching.[5]

As it turned out, a teaching vacancy soon arose in Concord, and Thoreau, no doubt swept along by parental and societal expectations, as well as economic need, applied for and was offered a teaching position at the town school. Though he applied himself to this job, within a month he was taken aside by a member of the school committee and reprimanded for not caning disruptive students, which was the school policy and apparently beyond negotiation. In protest to what he considered the absurdity of corporal punishment, Thoreau re-entered the classroom, randomly selected six students, administered to them a caning, then resigned. [6]

With his principles intact (somewhat dubiously, perhaps) but without a job, Thoreau's crisis of vocation deepened. There was some temporary respite when he and his brother established their own Concord Academy, a private school which ran quite successfully for a couple of years. But by March 1941 the project was abandoned and the vocational crisis re-emerged, as he was not particularly drawn to teaching. Over the next few years, lacking any clear direction, Thoreau found himself periodically employed in a variety of miscellaneous roles, including labourer, pencil-maker, gardener and general handyman at the Emerson residence, tutor for Emerson's nephew, occasional lecturer, and editor.

During this time, directionless though it may have seemed to others, Thoreau nevertheless came to understand with increasing certainty what he needed to do and what he had always wanted to be. As Carl Bode put it: 'He believed that his job was to become a writer but a writer in a noble Transcendentalist way – a poet first in what he did and next in what he wrote.'[7] The poet's noblest work, according to Thoreau's ambitious conception of the poet, was his life, and his poetry or prose would grow out of his life. [8]

The economic problem of how to support himself, however, was not yet solved. How was he to live as a poet – to follow his true calling – and still earn a living? It is a question, perhaps, to which we can all relate, in our own way. With some justification Thoreau considered it 'the most practically important of all questions,'[9] and yet when he sought out advice on how best to answer it he was surprised and disappointed by what he discovered:

> There is little or nothing to be remembered written on the subject of getting an honest living. Neither the New Testament nor Little Richard speaks to our condition. I cannot think of a single page which entertains, much less answers, the questions which I put to myself on this subject.... Is it that men are too disgusted with their experience to speak of it? Or that commonly they do not

question the common modes? The most practically important of all questions, it seems to me, is how shall I get my living, and yet I find nothing to my purpose in any book.... I consider that society with all its arts, has done nothing for us in this regard.[10]

Moreover, although he had just graduated from Harvard – an elite university even then – Thoreau came to realise that throughout his formal education there the question of *how to live* had been strangely passed over. Reflecting upon his studies, he felt as if he had been sent 'into the neighbourhood of some professor, where anything was professed and practiced except the art of life.'[11] Typifying his educational experience, he was astonished to discover upon leaving college that he had studied navigation, claiming that if he had taken one turn down the harbour he would have known more about it.[12] It was all theory and no practice. As for economics, Thoreau's gripe was that, '[e]ven the *poor* student studies only *political* economy, while that economy of living which is synonymous with philosophy is not even sincerely professed in our colleges.'[13] The consequence of this for the student, he noted dryly, is that 'while he is reading Adam Smith, Ricardo, and Say, he runs his father in debt irretrievably.'[14] Needless to say, studying the classical economists had not solved Thoreau's economic problem of how to live poetically.

Feeling that books and his formal education had failed him in this crucial way, Thoreau turned his attention to his contemporaries, the people of Concord, to see whether their lives could provide him with some insight into the art of living well, the art of freedom. His observations, however, far from showing him the way, instead gave rise to one of the most penetrating critiques of materialistic culture that has ever been laid down, one all the more piercing due to the fact that Thoreau was both a ruthless critic and a literary genius.

Only by examining this critique can we understand what ultimately drove Thoreau out of his township and into the woods.

1.2. *Thoreau on Materialistic Culture*

'Let us consider the way in which we spend our lives,' Thoreau began one of his essays, noting that since time was short he would 'leave out all the flattery, and retain all the criticism,'[15] as was his way. 'What is it to be born free and not to live free?' he asked his fellow citizens. 'Is it a freedom to be slaves, or a freedom to be free, of which we boast?' America may have been free from political tyrants, but it was painfully clear to Thoreau that it was 'still the slave of an economical and moral tyrant.'[16] A tyrant called Mammon.

This world is a place of 'incessant business,' he lamented, and there is 'nothing, not even crime, more opposed to poetry, to philosophy, ay, to life itself, than this incessant business.'[17] He felt that 'It would be glorious to see mankind at leisure for once,' but there is 'nothing but work, work, work.'[18] To be sure, Thoreau was not opposed to labour, industry, or enterprise, as such. His concern, rather, was that the ways by which money is acquired 'almost without exception lead downward,'[19] almost always involve 'lying, flattering, voting, contracting yourself into a nutshell of civility, or dilating into an atmosphere of thin and vaporous generosity, that you may persuade your neighbor to let you make his shoes, or his hat, or his coat, or his carriage, or import his groceries for him.'[20] And 'those services which the community will most readily pay for, it is most disagreeable to render.'[21] Thus, 'It is not enough to [say] that you worked hard to get your gold. So does the Devil work hard.'[22]

For these reasons Thoreau thought that to do anything merely for the sake of acquiring money or material superfluities was to be 'truly idle or worse.'[23] The following passage states his position directly:

> If I should sell my forenoons and afternoons to society, as most appear to do, I am sure that for me there would be nothing left worth living for.... I wish to suggest that a man may be very industrious, and yet not spend his time well. There is no more fatal blunderer than he who consumes the greater part of his life getting his living.[24]

But Thoreau saw his townsfolk labouring under this very mistake. 'It is a fool's life,' he asserted bluntly, 'as they will find when they get to the end of it, if not before.'[25] He had travelled widely in Concord, and everywhere, in shops, offices, and fields, the inhabitants seemed to him to be leading lives of 'quiet desperation' and doing penance in a thousand remarkable ways. 'The twelve labors of Hercules were trifling in comparison with those which my neighbors have undertaken; for they were only twelve, and had an end; but I could never see that these men slew or captured any monster or finished any labor.'[26] Thoreau likened people's materialistic cravings to the heads of a hydra, noting that 'as soon as one head is crushed, two spring up.'[27]

The ancient Chinese philosopher Lao Tzu once said, 'Those who know they have enough are rich.'[28] Thoreau was telling his contemporaries that they had 'enough' but that they did not know it, and so were poor. Always wanting more luxuries and comforts and never content with less, he felt that they did not understand the meaning of 'economy,' did not understand that the 'cost of a thing is the amount of... life which is required to be exchanged for it.'[29] 'Most men,' he wrote, 'even in this comparatively free country, through mere ignorance or mistake, are so occupied with factitious cares and superfluously course labors of life that its finer fruits cannot be plucked by them.'[30] By a 'seeming fate,' there was 'no time to be anything but a machine.'[31]

And for what? People's lives were being 'ploughed into the soil for compost'[32] just to obtain 'splendid houses' and 'finer and more abundant clothing... and the like.' But as Thoreau insisted, 'Superfluous wealth can buy superfluities only.'[33] Indeed, he claimed that 'Most of the luxuries, and many of the so-called comforts of life, are not only not indispensable, but positive hindrances to the elevation of mankind.'[34] Thoreau was astounded by how 'frivolous' people were with respect to their own lives, more concerned about accumulating nice things or climbing the social ladder than they were about their own destinies – as if they could 'kill time without injuring eternity.'[35]

'Who made them serfs of the soil?' he asked, again implying that his contemporaries were slaves to their uncontained material desires and yet oblivious to this self-imposed servitude. 'It is hard to have a Southern overseer; it is worse to have a Northern one; but worst of all when you are the slave-driver of yourself.' At the height of his indignation Thoreau even turned on the abolitionists, and told them: 'Ye are all slaves.'[36] This was no mere rhetorical gesture. One of his poems even mocks the abolitionists' vehemence:

> Make haste & set the captive free! –
> Are ye so free that cry?
> The lowest depths of slavery
> Leave freedom for a sigh.[37]

The English poet William Wordsworth penned the lines 'Getting and spending, we lay waste our powers,'[38] and we can imagine Thoreau being wholly sympathetic to this critical sentiment. And yet, such uncompromising condemnation of profit-seeking and acquisitiveness, of what Thoreau called 'the commercial spirit,' may give rise to the objection that Thoreau and Wordsworth were just disaffected romantics who failed to appreciate what were arguably the many *beneficial* aspects of industrial capitalism. Thoreau, however, had anticipated this retort: '"What!" exclaim a million Irishmen starting up from all the shanties in the land, "is not this railroad which we have built a good thing?" Yes, I answer, *comparatively* good, that is, you might have done worse; but I wish, as you are brothers of mine, that you could have spent your time better than digging in this dirt.'[39] 'As for the Pyramids,' Thoreau remarked, inviting us to reconsider the nature of human industry, 'there is nothing to wonder at in them so much as the fact that so many men could be found degraded enough to spend their lives constructing a tomb for some ambitious booby, whom it would have been wiser and manlier to have drowned in the Nile, and then given his body to the dogs. I might possibly invent some excuse for them and him, but I have not time for it.'[40] It was much the same for the United States Bank, Thoreau concluded. 'It costs more than it comes to,'[41] in terms of *life*, a calculus to which we will return.

Thoreau was living in a time of great economic transformation and for him the railroad was the emblem of industrialisation. He often spoke of it metaphorically, as a representation of the emerging economic system that was fast changing the face of America and indeed the world. 'We do not ride upon the railroad,' he asserted, 'it rides upon us.'[42] He developed this image in the following memorable passage:

> Did you ever think what those sleepers are that underlie the railroad? Each one is a man, an Irishman, or a Yankee man. The rails are laid on them, and they are covered with sand, and the cars run smoothly over them. They are sound sleepers, I assure you. And every few years a new lot is laid down and run over; so that, if some have the pleasure of riding upon a rail, others have the misfortune to be ridden upon. And when they run over a man that is walking in his sleep... and wake him up, they suddenly stop the cars, and make a hue and cry about it, as if this were an exception. I am glad to know that it takes a gang of men for every five miles to keep the sleepers down and level in their beds as it is, for this is a sign that they may sometime get up again.[43]

Thoreau indeed hoped that those 'sleepers' who were being ridden upon by industrialisation would 'sometime get up again,' and he did what he could to wake his neighbors up.[44] But it appeared to Thoreau as if his sleeping neighbours had fallen into the common mode of living not because they preferred it to any other, but because they honestly thought there was no choice left. 'So thoroughly and sincerely are we compelled to live, reverencing our life, and denying the possibility of change. This is the only way, we say.'[45]

But Thoreau was not convinced. He was of the view that 'there are as many ways as there can be drawn radii from one center.'[46] 'Here is life, an experiment to a great extent untried by me; but it does not avail me that they have tried it... [M]an's capacities have never been measured; nor are we to judge of what he can do by any precedents, so little has been tried.'[47] Even 'the life which men praise and regard as successful is but one kind,' and 'why should we exaggerate any one kind at the expense of the others?'[48] Forever the thoughtful non-conformist, Thoreau tended to believe that, 'What old people say you cannot do you try and find that you can,' and on that basis he boldly proposed that there should be, 'Old deeds for old people, and new deeds for new.'[49]

It was time for Thoreau to begin his living experiment at Walden Pond.

1.3. *The Walden Experiment*

On Independence Day, 1845, a few days before his twenty-eighth birthday, Henry Thoreau left his town of Concord and went to live alone in the woods, on the shores of Walden Pond, a mile from any neighbour. He there built himself a modest cabin and for two years and two months earned a simple living by the labour of his own hands. He also wrote, among other things, his autobiographical masterpiece, *Walden: Life in the Woods*, which gives a philosophical and literary account of his two-year stay. This is arguably the greatest statement ever made on the living strategy now variously known as 'voluntary simplicity,' 'simple living,' or 'downshifting.'[50]

In the second chapter of *Walden*, entitled 'Where I Lived, and What I Lived For,' Thoreau offers us an explanation for his exit from conventional society: 'I went the woods because I wished to live deliberately, to front only the essential facts of life and see if I could not learn what they had to teach, and not, when I came to die, discover that I had not lived.'[51] He 'did not wish to live what was not life,' he tells us, 'living is so dear;' nor did he wish to 'practice resignation, unless it was quite necessary.'[52]

> I wanted to live deep and suck out all the marrow of life, to live so sturdily and Spartan-like as to put to rout all that was not life,... to drive life into a corner, and reduce it to its lowest terms, and, if it proved to be mean, why then to get the whole and genuine meanness out of it, and publish its meanness to the world; or if it was sublime, to know it by experience.[53]

Elsewhere he said that his purpose in going to Walden Pond was to 'transact some private business with the fewest obstacles.'[54] In one sense, this 'private business' was simply to write in solitude, close to Nature and away from distractions.[55] In another sense, though closely related to the first, his 'private business' was to solve, or at least better understand, the economic problem of how to live poetically in a world of scarce resources. Perhaps, Thoreau had decided, the best path was to reduce his material wants and live a simple life. He thought that 'it would be some advantage to live a primitive and frontier life, though in the midst of an outward civilisation, if only to learn what are the gross necessaries of life and what methods have been taken to obtain them.'[56] Simplicity of life was to be his means to the elevation of purpose.

Thoreau had come to suspect that if one's trade were with the 'Celestial Empire'[57] – by which he meant, 'If your concerns are "higher" than merely getting and spending' – then very little is actually needed to live well and to be free, provided life is approached with the right attitude. 'Simplify, simplify,'[58] was to become his refrain. A modest shelter from the elements should be fixture enough. Old clothes will do, will they not? 'Instead of three meals a day, if it be necessary eat but one; instead of a hundred dishes, five; and reduce other things in proportion.'[59] Most importantly, 'keep your accounts on your thumbnail.'[60]

This, in essence, was the method Thoreau put to the test at Walden Pond, by living simply and rejecting the division of labour. As far as possible he secured his own food, by growing beans, peas, corn, turnips, and potatoes, and occasionally fishing in the pond. He cut down some local trees and built himself a house with but one small room, and made some basic furniture. It was not much, but it was enough. And just enough was plenty. He did not wish to be chained to the economy, so he practiced self-reliance; he did not wish to be slave to artificial material desires, so he practiced self-discipline; and he did not wish to live what was not life, so he practiced self-culture. In short, he practiced what I am calling 'alternative economics.'

The economic significance of Thoreau's life in the woods can only be understood if we always keep in mind what he was trying to accomplish there. As noted above, Thoreau wanted to be a writer in the Transcendentalist sense, a poet not just of words but of his life; which is to say, he wanted to infuse his everyday affairs with his highest goals and yield to 'all the impulses of the soul.'[61] By 1845, however, it had become clear to this Transcendentalist that his 'private business' was not likely to procure him even a moderate allowance in the market. 'For a long time,' he noted, 'I was reporter to a journal, of no very wide circulation, whose editor has never yet seen fit to print the bulk of my contributions, and, as is too common with writers, I got only my labor for my pains.'[62] Indeed, we have seen that Thoreau, in the eight years between his graduation from Harvard and his excursion to the pond, struggled in vain to find an occupation which would not conflict with the activities that yielded his poems and essays.[63] His options, it seemed, were either to make some compromises and pursue a different vocation – that is, to do something for which there was much more demand in the market – or else somehow find a way to become much less dependent on the market. In the following parable, which I will quote at length due to the centrality of the point it expresses, Thoreau neatly captures the essence both of his economic situation and his response to it:

> Not long since, a strolling Indian went to sell baskets at the house of a well-known lawyer in my neighborhood. 'Do you wish to buy any baskets?' he asked. 'No, we do not want any,' was the reply. 'What!' exclaimed the Indian as he went out the gate, 'do you mean to starve us?' Having seen his industrious white neighbors so well off – that the lawyer had only to weave arguments, and, by some magic, wealth and standing followed – he had said to himself: I will go into business; I will weave baskets; it is a thing which I can do. Thinking that when he had made the baskets he would have done his part, and then it would be the white man's to buy them. He had not discovered that it was necessary for him to make it worth the other's while to buy them, or at least make him think that it was so, or to make something else which it would be worth his while to buy. I too had woven a kind of basket of a delicate texture, but I had not made it worth any one's while to buy them. Yet not the less, in my case, did I think it worth my while to weave them, and instead of studying how to make it worth men's while to buy my baskets, I studied rather how to avoid the necessity of selling them.[64]

Before moving on to consider this 'study' of Thoreau's in some detail, the fruits of which are his alternative economics, I wish to take a moment to ensure that Thoreau is not misunderstood on one very important point. Whatever his neighbours may have thought, Thoreau's venture into the woods was not an attempt to escape reality or to escape what may have been his duties. On the contrary, he knew it to be a journey toward reality and an undertaking to meet his duties; in particular, the duty to take his deepest aspirations seriously. 'As I preferred some things to others,' he wrote, 'and especially valued my freedom, ... I did not wish to spend my time in earning rich carpets or other fine furniture, or delicate cookery, or a house in the Grecian or the Gothic style just yet. If there are any to whom it is no interruption [to their 'proper pursuits'] to acquire these things, and who know how to use them when acquired, I relinquish to them the pursuit.'[65] Thoreau was clearly terrified of falling into the ruts of tradition and conformity, of compromising his dreams and wasting life in the pursuit of trivial luxuries, as he saw so many of his contemporaries doing and which he considered to be 'not so sad as foolish.'[66] He knew that he would not be able to pluck life's 'finer fruits' if he devoted too much of his time to the 'coarse labors of life,' and so he set about lowering his denominator, reducing his needs.[67] Thoreau's experiment with simplicity, then, was not a renunciation of life, but an affirmation of it. He found the gift of life to be glorious, and for that reason was 'anxious to improve the nick of time, and notch it on to [his] stick; to stand on the meeting of two eternities, the past and the future, which is precisely the present moment; to toe that line.'[68] To this passage he added: 'You will pardon some obscurities, for there are more secrets in my trade than in most men's, and yet not voluntarily kept, but inseparable from its very nature.'[69]

Thoreau wanted to live without dead time, and he went to Walden Pond to learn how to achieve this; or, at least, to see if it were possible. As a matter of principle, it seemed, he would not accept any division of his day between lower and higher aims, between ordinary and poetic experience. This is what it means to live efficiently, to live economically, in Thoreau's sense. This is a very different approach, it must be said, to that of mainstream economic thought, which generally assumes that to live efficiently or act economically means 'maximising wealth,'[70] evaluated in terms of dollars. And thus Thoreau's economics are 'alternative' in the sense that economic success is measured not with such yardsticks as productive labour (e.g., Adam Smith) or money (e.g., Richard Posner), but with the yardstick of a life lived well, a life lived deliberately. Admittedly, this may be more difficult to quantify than money or labour, but only with this alternative yardstick in mind can we understand what Thoreau meant when he stated, 'I have always endeavoured to acquire strict business habits; they are indispensable to every man,'[71] and why he thought that 'Walden Pond would be a good place for business.'[72] His business was not to make money but to become a 'Transcendental Capitalist'[73] who trades with the 'Celestial Empire.' The following passage exemplifies Thoreau's radically unconventional conception of good business:

> Sometimes, in a summer morning, having taken my accustomed bath [in the pond], I sat in my sunny doorway from sunrise till noon, rapt in a revery, amidst the pines and the hickories and sumachs, in undisturbed solitude and stillness, while the birds sang around or flitted noiseless through the house, until by the sun's falling in at my west window, or the noise of some traveler's wagon on the distant highway, I was reminded of the lapse of time. I grew in those seasons like corn in the night, and they were far better than any work of the hands would have been.[74]

To the people of Concord, 'this was sheer idleness... no doubt.'[75] But Thoreau was sure that 'if the birds and flowers had tried [him] by their standard, [he] should not have been found wanting.'[76] As he was to write in his journal: 'If it is not poetic, it is not life but death we get.'[77]

In the above passages about 'business,' and indeed throughout *Walden* at every opportunity, Thoreau conveys the joys of a 'higher and more ethereal life,'[78] a 'spiritual view of things,'[79] with the language of economics and commerce. He does this to provoke us, to unsettle us in our judgements of life, by parodying conventional means of evaluation, by making outrageous comparisons, and by mocking those who measure things in life 'by the... dollar only.'[80] Stanley Cavell, in his celebrated study *The Senses of Walden*, talks of how Thoreau employs a 'maze' of economic terms, including 'money,... profit and loss, rich and poor, cost and expense, borrow and pay, owe and own, business, commerce, enterprises, ventures, affairs, capital, price, amount, improvement, bargain, employment, inheritance, bankruptcy, work, trade, labor, idle, spend, waste, allowance, fortune, gain, earn, afford, possession, change, settling, living, interest, prospects, means, terms.'[81] And as another commentator notes, Thoreau uses this vast imagery 'to expose the insidious control exerted over our lives by the economic system of profit and loss which we so easily take for granted,... to demonstrate how overwhelmingly our vision of life is dominated by commercial values.'[82] Put otherwise, Thoreau tries to help us escape the capitalist semantics that have infiltrated our vocabulary and which have come to shape the way we see the world and our place in it. His strategy is to use familiar economic concepts in unfamiliar, even shocking, ways. This strategy is epitomised by his claim that there were days at the pond, 'when idleness was the most attractive and productive industry. Many a forenoon have I have stolen away, preferring to spend thus the most valuable part of the day; for I was rich, if not in money, in sunny hours and summer days, and spent them lavishly; nor do I regret that I did not waste more of them in the workshop or at the teacher's desk.'[83]

By defining 'the cost of a thing' as 'the amount of what I will call life which is required to be exchanged for it,'[84] Thoreau inverts the values of conventional economics, making life – instead of the dollar-value of commodities – the highest good. Life, he suggests, consists of a limited amount of time, energy, and attention, which may be conserved, saved, spent, employed, stolen, squandered, or hoarded – just like property.[85] This inverted value-system forms the basis of Thoreau's alternative economics.

2. THOREAU'S ALTERNATIVE ECONOMICS

It is now time to take a closer look at how exactly Thoreau set about answering the economic questions that confronted him; questions, I have suggested, which will confront any whose true calling happens to have little value in the market. *How best to earn a living? How much time should I spend at it? How much do I need to live well and to be free?* Thoreau had discovered that there was an incompatibility between his self-culture and a profit-centred civilisation, but instead of studying how to sell the product of his genius in the market, remember, Thoreau studied how to avoid the necessity of selling it. For as he was to say with characteristic disdain, 'trade curses everything it handles.'[86]

With the groundwork complete, let us make haste to Thoreau's living experiment. We will begin with his discussion of the 'necessaries of life': what they are, how they are best understood, and what questions arise upon obtaining them. We will then examine Thoreau's perspective on what lies beyond the necessaries of life, those material things which can be broadly categorised into comforts, luxuries, or tools. We will also consider Thoreau's thoughts on two other miscellaneous subjects: technology and working hours. Finally, we will inquire into why Thoreau might have left Walden Pond and whether or not his living experiment can be judged a success.[87]

2.1. *The Necessaries of Life*

The first task set by alternative economics is to determine what are the gross necessaries of life, 'for not till we have secured these are we prepared to entertain the true problems of life with freedom and a prospect of success.'[88] The quoted passage is important because with it Thoreau is seeking to avoid a misunderstanding that might arise, and sometimes does, from his celebration of material simplicity. Simplicity is not material destitution, he is saying. We all have basic physical needs that have to be met (though they may be fewer than we commonly think). If those needs are not met then we would be consumed by anxiety over where our next meal might come from or whether we would be able to survive the cold night. And that is obviously not a condition conducive to a life of freedom, a flourishing life. Accordingly, before dedicating any of our energies to marvelling at the wonders of the world, to developing our higher capacities, or to composing novel, personally meaningful answers to the questions posed by human existence, we will need to secure at least a certain minimum of material things to ensure our healthy, physical subsistence. Securing that minimum is therefore of immediate and primary importance.[89]

By the words, *necessaries of life*, Thoreau meant 'whatever... has been from the first, or from long use has become, so important to human life that few, if any... ever attempt to do without.'[90] Although most creatures have only food as a true necessary of life, and perhaps shelter, also, Thoreau held that the necessaries of life for a human being in his climate 'may, accurately enough, be distributed under the several heads of Food, Shelter, Clothing, and Fuel.'[91] In the following sections I discuss these necessaries of life from the critical perspective of Thoreau's alternative economics, following the order in which he discusses them in 'Economy,' the first chapter of *Walden*. I will, however, defer the discussion of Fuel, since it is largely metaphorical and is best addressed later. (In any case, there is little to discuss, factually; the woods provided Thoreau with ample fuel for his fire.)

2.2. Clothing

With respect to procuring clothing, Thoreau wondered whether we are more often led by the love of novelty and the opinions of others, than by a true utility. 'We worship not the Graces... but Fashion. The head monkey at Paris puts on a traveler's cap, and all the monkeys in America do the same.'[92] This taste for 'new patterns,' Thoreau complained, is 'childish and savage,'[93] by in large a waste of our vital energy and attention. What is worse, '[t]he manufacturers have learned that this taste is merely whimsical. Of two patterns which differ only by a few threads more or less of a particular colour, the one will be sold readily, the other lie on the shelf, though it frequently happens that after the lapse of a season the latter becomes the most fashionable.'[94] Worse still, however, is that the principal object of the factory system 'is not that mankind may be well and honestly clad but, unquestionably, that the corporations may be enriched.'[95] One could be forgiven for thinking that Thoreau was writing in the 21st century.

Another criticism Thoreau levelled at the institution of 'fashion' is that it is largely out of our control, at least in terms of what is in vogue. It follows that if we choose to respect fashion (and Thoreau would insist that it is a choice) we thereby hand over some of our powers and freedoms, as well as our capacity for aesthetic judgement, to a highly dubious ruler – that monkey in Paris. Thoreau, for one, would not be ruled by a monkey:

> When I ask for a garment of a particular form, my tailoress tells me gravely, 'They do not make them so now,' not emphasizing the 'They' at all, as if she quoted an authority as impersonal as the Fates, and I find it difficult to get made what I want, simply because she cannot believe that I mean what I say, that I am so rash. When I hear this oracular sentence, I am for a moment absorbed in thought, emphasizing to myself each word separately that I may come at the meaning of it, that I may find out by what degree of consanguinity *They* are related to *me*, and what authority they may have in an affair which affects me so nearly; and, finally, I am inclined to answer her with equal mystery, and without any more emphasis of the 'they' – 'It is true, they did not make them so recently, but they do now.'[96]

Thoreau reminds us that 'the object of clothing is, first, to retain the vital heat, and secondly, in this state of society, to cover nakedness.'[97] On that basis he suggested – and this is his central point here – that any necessary or important work may be accomplished without adding to our wardrobes. 'A man who has at length found something to do will not need to get a new suit to do it in.'[98] Beware, then, he wrote, 'of all enterprises that require new clothes, and not rather the new wearer of clothes.'[99]

Thoreau was of the view that, in terms of what is necessary to life, functional clothing can be obtained very cheaply – 'at prices to suit customers really'[100] – or even made at home for a nominal cost. Furthermore, he thought that before we seek 'finer clothing' we should first make sure that our pursuits are 'finer,' or else we are just relying on the 'false skin' of clothing to obtain a false respect.[101] Thoreau wondered how far people would retain their relative rank if they were divested of their clothes. Should this happen, he implied, we would simply have to confer social status on the basis of *worthiness*, or the like, rather than on the basis of fine dress, which all too often merely represents an accidental and arbitrary possession of wealth.

What should it matter, in the greater scheme of things, if we have to dress in last season's colours or wear a patch over the knee? 'Most behave as if they would be ruined if they should do it. It would be easier for them to hobble to town with a broken leg than with a broken pantaloon.'[102] But, wrote Thoreau: 'No man ever stood the lower in my estimation for having a patch on his clothes; yet I am sure that there is greater anxiety, commonly, to have fashionable, or at least clean and unpatched clothes, than to have a sound conscience.'[103]

Bringing his argument to a head, Thoreau stated: 'Only those who go to soirees and legislative halls must have new coats, coats to change as often as the man changes in them. But if my jacket and trousers, my hat and shoes, are fit to worship God in, they will do, will they not?'[104] It is an interesting question to consider, if not in relation to the worship of God, necessarily, then more generally in relation to the living of a passionate life. Old clothes will do, will they not? Thoreau proposed that they will do just fine.

We might donate our old, superfluous clothing to those poorer than ourselves, but we might then find Thoreau telling us that, in terms of clothing, at least, the poor are actually richer than us for being able to do with less. But Thoreau must not be misunderstood here. He is not glorifying the poor or prescribing to us a dress code. He is attempting to get us to reconsider cultural assumptions about the importance of material things (in this case clothing) to a well-lived life. His argument is not that one cannot live a happy and meaningful life in fine clothing so much as fine clothing is not necessary for a happy and meaningful life. If that is so, reducing the consumption of fine clothing should not negatively affect overall wellbeing. In fact, since reducing consumption in clothing implies a correlative reduction in the labour needed to produce clothing, wellbeing is likely to increase since less time labouring means more leisure time – more freedom.

2.3. *Shelter*

As for shelter, Thoreau does not deny that this is now a necessary of life, though he does make a point of noting that there are instances of human beings, no hardier than ourselves, doing without shelter for long periods in colder countries.[105] Assuming, however, that shelter is indeed a necessary of life, Thoreau proposed that we '[c]onsider first how slight a shelter is absolutely necessary.'[106] He had seen Indians in his town living in tents of thin cotton cloth, which in the first instance could be constructed in a day or two, at most, and taken down and put up in a few hours; and every family owned one.[107] He had even seen a large box by the railroad, six feet long by three feet wide, in which the labourers locked their tools up at night, and it suggested to him that anyone who was hard pushed might get such a one for a dollar, and, having bored a few holes in it to admit the air at least, get into it when it rained at night, and hook down the lid, 'and so have freedom in his love, and in his soul be free.'[108] This will strike some as a ridiculous proposition, but Thoreau was 'far from jesting.'[109] An average house in his neighbourhood cost about eight hundred dollars at the time and Thoreau noted that to lay up this sum would take from ten to fifteen years of the labourer's life; add the farm and one would have to spend twenty, thirty, or forty years toiling – more than half of one's life is easily spent. Would the Indians have been wise to give up their tents on these terms?

It is in this context where Thoreau made his alternative economics most explicit, expressing the core idea which we have already considered and, for emphasis, will consider again. 'If it is asserted that civilization is a real advance in the condition of man – and I think it is, though only the wise improve their advantages – it must be shown that it has produced better dwellings without making them more costly; and the cost of a thing is the amount of life which is required to be exchanged for it, immediately or in the long run.'[110] On this basis, Thoreau suggested that 'when the farmer has got his house, he may not be the richer but the poorer for it, and it be the house that has got him.'[111] What is more, *'if the civilized man's pursuits are no worthier than the savage's, if he is employed the greater part of his life in obtaining gross necessaries and comforts merely, why should he have a better dwelling than the former?'*[112]

Thoreau wanted to show at what sacrifice our more 'advanced' dwellings were obtained and to suggest that, by living more simply, we may secure all the advantage without suffering any of the disadvantage. With this in mind, he went to Walden Pond with an axe, cut down some trees, and in about three unrushed months had built himself a modest but sturdy cabin. Again exemplifying his alternative mode of economic analysis, Thoreau declared that, 'I intend to build me a house which will surpass any on the main street in Concord in grandeur and luxury, as soon as it pleases me as much and will cost me no more [in terms of life] than the present one.'[113]

It appears, then, that Thoreau was *perfectly content* with his shelter, modest though it was. Did this not make him richer than a king who is dissatisfied with his palace? With a little more wit we could *all* be richer than kings, Thoreau implied; but, unfortunately: 'Most men appear never to have considered what a house is, and are actually though needlessly poor all their lives because they think that they must have such a one as their neighbors have.'[114]

Furthermore, Thoreau thought that there is something important in the *experience* of providing for oneself, of being self-reliant, that has been lost as a result of so-called 'modern improvements' and capitalism's extreme division of labour. He wondered whether 'if men constructed their dwellings with their own hands... the poetic faculty would be universally developed, as birds universally sing when they are so engaged?'[115] But, alas, 'we do like cowbirds and cuckoos, which lay their eggs in nests which other birds have built.'[116]

'Shall we forever resign the pleasure of construction to the carpenter?'[117] he asked, noting that never in all his walks had he come across anyone engaged in so simple and natural an occupation as building their own house. 'Where is [our] division of labor to end? And what object does it finally serve? No doubt another *may* also think for me; but it is not therefore desirable that he should do so to the exclusion of my thinking for myself.'[118] Thoreau had come to believe that his contemporaries were endeavouring to solve the problem of their livelihoods by a formula more complicated than the problem itself. 'To get his shoestrings he speculates in herds of cattle.'[119] But Thoreau showed that, if one is prepared to live simply and with more self-reliance, 'the student who wishes for a shelter can obtain one for a lifetime at an expense not greater than the rent which he now pays annually,'[120] and 'become richer than the richest are now.'[121]

Thoreau's calculus here is essentially the same as it was regarding clothing. Perhaps it would be nice to live in a palace or a mansion or even the nicest house on the block, but it must not be forgotten that the more expensive one's housing is the more of one's life one will probably have to spend earning the money needed to buy or rent it (assuming we are not kings or queens). So why not keep housing modest and simple? Since housing is the greatest overall expense in most people's lives, this is an area where people should be particularly cognisant of the time / freedom cost of consumption. Perhaps by lowering 'standard of living' (measured by consumption in housing) people could actually increase 'quality of life' (measured by subjective wellbeing)? Indeed, Thoreau's suggestion is that by living in modest accommodation people can literally save years if not decades of labour and thereby become 'richer than the richest are now,' not in terms of property, of course, but in terms of freedom and contentment. 'If I seem to boast more than is becoming,' he concluded, 'my excuse is that I brag for humanity rather than for myself.'[122]

2.4. Food

During his two-year stay at the pond, as noted earlier, Thoreau grew for himself the bulk of the food he ate – beans, especially, but also a few rows of peas, corn, turnips, and potatoes. He drank water. From this experience he learned, among other things, that it 'cost incredibly little trouble to obtain one's necessary food' and that 'a man may use as simple a diet as the animals, and yet retain health and strength.'[123] Reflecting on his first year of homesteading, Thoreau wrote that, '[a]ll things considered, that is, considering the importance of a man's soul and of today, ... I believe that [I] was doing better than any farmer in Concord.'[124] As well as providing for his own dietary needs, he also cultivated approximately two and half acres of beans which he later sold to meet his occasional miscellaneous expenses. [125] As for his second year:

> ... I did better still, for I spaded up all the land which I required, about a third of an acre, and I learned from the experience of both years, ... that if one would live simply and eat only the crop which he raised, and raise no more than he ate, and not exchange it for an insufficient quantity of more luxurious and expensive things, he would need to cultivate only a few rods of ground, and that it would be cheaper to spade up that than to use oxen to plow it, and to select a fresh spot from time to time than to manure the old, and he could do all his necessary farm work as it were with his left hand at odd hours in the summer. [126]

By simplifying his life and practicing self-reliance, Thoreau believed that he was more independent than any farmer he knew. 'I was not anchored to a house or farm, but could follow the bent of my genius, which is a very crooked one, every moment.' [127] This passage is significant because it shows that Thoreau's living experiment was meeting with some real success. He had gone into the woods, after all, to confront that 'vexed question' [128] of how to earn an honest living and still have freedom for his proper pursuits, and a life of simplicity and self-reliance was proving to be a promising response. Growing his own food, we see, was an important part of that response.

Growing his own food, however, came to be something much more than a matter of physically sustaining himself. In a chapter of *Walden* entitled 'The Bean Field' we find Thoreau telling us that:

> I came to love my rows, my beans... They attached me to the earth, and so I got strength like Antæus. But why should I raise them? Only Heaven knows. This was my curious labor all summer — to make this portion of the earth's surface, which had yielded only cinquefoil, blackberries, johnswort, and the like, before, sweet wild fruits and pleasant flowers, produce instead this pulse. What shall I learn of beans or beans of me? I cherish them, I hoe them, early and late I have an eye to them; and this is my day's work. [129]

Some readers may be reminded here of the passage by Nathaniel Hawthorne in which he talks with similar devotion about his own vegetable garden:

> I used to visit and revisit it a dozen times a day, and stand in deep contemplation over my vegetable progeny with a love that nobody could share or conceive of who had never taken part in the process of creation. It was one of the most bewitching sights in the world to observe a hill of beans thrusting aside the soil, or a rose of early peas just peeping forth sufficiently to trace a line of delicate green. [130]

Thoreau admitted that, since he had little aid from horses, cattle, or hired labour, or from the latest farming implements, he was 'much slower' in his work than other farmers. [131] Nevertheless, he claimed that he became much more 'intimate' with his beans on this account and that his slower more personal approach yielded a 'constant and imperishable moral.' [132] This moral, he seemed to think, was that the fastest and most efficient way of farming, that is, the way that would yield the most profit in the market, was not necessarily the best way, all things considered. As Philip Cafaro has noted, Thoreau 'makes a point of doing most of the work himself, rather than contracting it out to more productive specialists with more elaborate tools. He does not, he tells us, bother with "imported" fertilisers. These moves would increase his productivity, but he refuses to allow that to dictate how he will farm.' [133] Furthermore, Thoreau could have hired himself out as a day labourer and for much less effort been able to buy his food at the grocers, but he chose not to. Doing so would have left him relying on others first to hire him and second to produce and then sell him his necessaries.

But Thoreau's reasons for living simply go deeper even than securing his independence and freedom. Allowing others to grow food for him, even if it was more 'efficient' or 'economic' to do so, would also have disconnected him from the land, from direct contact with Nature, that is, from the elemental source of both his material and spiritual nourishment. And Thoreau would have no truck with that. He did not just want the beans to eat; he also wanted the *experience* of cultivating them. In 'The Bean Field' we get an insight into the nature of his labours. Being outside, he tells us, working up a sweat under the morning sun and sky, hoeing his beans in the fresh country air, 'yielded an instant and immeasurable crop.'[134] At such times, he noted somewhat cryptically, it 'was no longer beans that I hoed,'[135] suggesting, we can suppose, that he was cultivating not so much the land as his own soul.

Thoreau delighted at being 'part and parcel of Nature.'[136] The chickadees became so familiar with him that at length one even perched upon an armful of wood which he was carrying, pecking at the sticks without fear. 'I once had a sparrow alight upon my shoulder for a moment while I was hoeing... and I felt that I was more distinguished by that circumstance than I should have been by an epaulet I could have worn. The squirrels also grew at last to be quite familiar, and occasionally stepped upon my shoe when that was the nearest way.'[137] Thoreau would listen to the brown thrashers as he worked his rows and would carefully observe the wildlife on the edge of his field. As he was not driven by an urge to maximise profits, and was thus in no real hurry, he could rest on his hoe and watch the hen-hawks circling high in the sky, 'alternately soaring and descending, approaching and leaving one another, as if they were the embodiment of my own thoughts.'[138] Philip Cafaro, again, captures the significance of these and similar experiences exactly: 'To a poet-naturalist, opportunities for such encounters, even opportunities to feel changes in the weather and mark the natural course of the day, are strengthening and vivifying. Thoreau contrasts this work with factory and office work, suggesting again that the experience lost is not made up in increased pay or productivity.'[139]

This Thoreauvian calculus deserves our most serious consideration, today more than ever before. But it will take some concerted imaginative effort on our part to broaden our view of things, since Thoreau suggested that we entrenched urbanites, who are highly dependent on the grocer and who live and work mostly indoors, can barely comprehend what it could even mean to be 'part and parcel with Nature.' And until we have some sense of its richness, some sense that there is another, simpler, more intimate way to provide for ourselves, we are likely to continue doing economics in the usual, narrow fashion and structuring our lives accordingly, not even knowing what we have lost, or, rather, what the market economy and its division of labour has taken from us. 'This is the only way, we say.'[140]

I will close this section by referring to another rather cryptic passage in *Walden*, in which Thoreau summarily dismisses all those timid souls who have doubts about the feasibility of alternative economics:

> There is a certain class of unbelievers who sometimes ask me such questions as, if I think that I can live on vegetable food alone; and to strike at the root of the matter at once – for the root is faith – I am accustomed to answer such, that I can live on board nails. If they cannot understand that, they cannot understand much that I have to say.[141]

3. BEYOND THE NECESSARIES: HOW MUCH IS ENOUGH?

So there we have it, the essence of Thoreau's views on clothing, shelter, and food. We saw that he also listed 'fuel' as a necessary of life, a need which he met easily by collecting the fallen branches from around his house and the driftwood from the pond, as well as by burning a few tree stumps.[142] What little else Thoreau said on the subject of fuel was metaphorical, as noted above, and we will see that his use of metaphor in this context leads us nicely onto our next subject, which concerns the nature of what lies *beyond* the necessaries of life.

Consider the following passage: 'By proper Shelter and Clothing we legitimately retain our own internal heat; but with an excess of these, or of Fuel, that is, with an external heat greater than our own internal, may not cookery properly be said to begin?'[143] Thoreau begins here by acknowledging, as he must, that a certain amount of the necessaries of life is 'legitimate' or 'proper,' but he then goes on to suggest that they will eventually stop serving any legitimate purpose and indeed detract from life if consumed in 'excess.' On the next page his suggestion becomes a statement: 'The luxuriously rich are not simply kept comfortably warm, but unnaturally hot; as I implied before, they are cooked, of course a la mode.'[144] Thoreau's metaphor implies that fire, like material wealth, is far from being an unqualified good in our lives, but is instead good or bad depending on how much of it there is and how it is used.

It is within this metaphor that Thoreau crafted one of the central passages in *Walden*:

> When a man is warmed by the several modes which I have described [i.e. Food, Shelter, Clothing, Fuel], what does he want next? Surely not more warmth of the same kind, as more and richer food, larger and more splendid houses, finer and more abundant clothing, more numerous, incessant, and hotter fires, and the like. When he has obtained those things which are necessary to life, there is another alternative than to obtain the superfluities; and that is, to adventure on life now, his vacation from humbler toil having commenced.[145]

Let us take some time to unpack Thoreau's insight here. The unstated background point is that we must first secure the necessaries of life, for without them we die. If their attainment means we have to toil all day in the humblest conditions, then toil we shall, for the sheer will to survive is a powerful driving force. When we have secured the necessaries of life, however, we are suddenly confronted by what Thoreau earlier called 'the true problems of life with freedom and a prospect of success.'[146] That is, we are faced with the question of whether to keep on pursuing material things beyond what is necessary or *to do something else with our lives*. Thoreau was so critical of his contemporaries because to him they rarely seemed to face this question and instead thoughtlessly spent their lives accumulating material 'superfluities' – richer foods, splendid houses, finer clothing, hotter fires, etc. – as if that were the only way to live. 'It is a fool's life,' we have heard him declare, 'as they will find when they get to the end of it if not before.'[147] But there is an alternative, Thoreau insisted, and that is 'to adventure on life now,' our 'vacation from humbler toil having commenced.' Suddenly switching to a new metaphor, Thoreau proposed that, having rooted ourselves firmly in the earth and secured our material foundations, like the seeds of noble plants we should now rise confidently toward the heavens.[148]

Thoreau is not proposing, however, that we only ever work to obtain the gross necessaries of life *and no more*. Put otherwise, he does not deny that there are times when obtaining more than is strictly necessary can genuinely improve our lives and help us achieve our goals (a point which we will consider further in a later section). But Thoreau is warning us not to assume that material wealth will always contribute positively to our lives, for often, in insidious ways, it will not. It is not that there is anything inherently evil about money or material things; it is just that each moment we spend pursuing such things beyond what is necessary is a moment we could have spent on some free, non-materialistic good – such as sauntering through the woods, in Thoreau's case – and we should always be cognisant of this type of trade-off. Sometimes trading our time for money and things will be a good trade, no doubt. But sometimes such a trade will ultimately cost more than it comes to in terms of *life*, making us not richer but poorer, and thus be a bad trade.

This calculus, as we have seen, is the heart of Thoreau's alternative economics. The essential lesson can be expressed as follows: *once we have obtained those things necessary to life, we should thereafter carefully assess how much more we actually need to live well and to be free, by thinking about whether the pursuit of more material things would actually improve or detract from our lives, immediately or in the long run, and act on that basis.*[149] Applying this calculus to our lives may not be easy or clear cut, especially in a culture that celebrates material wealth as a good in itself. But if we neglect it – if we just assume that more material wealth is what is needed to improve our lives – then we are at risk of getting cooked, of course a la mode. Those who do not want to be cooked must honestly confront the challenging question posed by Thoreau's alternative economics: 'How much material wealth is *enough*?'

◆ ◆ ◆

This question leads us to an unexpected twist in the narrative of alternative economics. We discover that it is impossible to answer the question, 'How much is enough?', until we have first answered a prior and even more important question: 'Enough for *what*?' This prior question challenges us to specify the point of our economic activity, for if we cannot identify its purpose we cannot know if our economic efforts have succeeded. Without some 'chief end' in mind to guide and justify our labour, we would merely be running in the ruts or acting for no conscious purpose, like the Brahmin who chained himself for life to the foot of a tree, but could not explain why he did it. [150] Thoreau is warning us, in effect, that if we do not have a clear sense of what we are doing with our lives, or why we are heading in one direction rather than another, we will not be able to tell if our attitudes toward material things are keeping us on the right path or leading us astray. In the next section we must take an apparent detour to consider this issue in more detail.

4. ENOUGH FOR *WHAT*? AN INTERLUDE ON SELF-CULTURE

It was the German philosopher, Friedrich Nietzsche, who proclaimed: 'Be the poet of your life.' [151] This imperative is one that we can be sure Thoreau would have received sympathetically, had he ever been exposed to it. [152] If we are prepared to broaden our conception of poetry to include more than just written or spoken verse, and define it (as did the romantic poet Percy Bysshe Shelly) as 'the expression of the imagination,' [153] then to say, 'be the poet of your life,' begins to make more sense. Blurring the distinction between art and life, it suggests that we should take hold of life, as the poet takes hold of language, and shape it into something worthy – to imagine the best life we can and then set about creating such a life. For are we not each related to our own lives in a way comparable to how the artist is related to his or her raw materials? [154] Are we not each charged with composing as an aesthetic project the meaning of our own lives? As Thoreau wrote: 'It is something to be able to paint a particular picture, or to carve a statue, and so make a few objects beautiful, but it is far more glorious to carve and paint the very atmosphere and medium through which we look.'[155] Similarly, in the conclusion to *Walden* he urged us all to 'live the life [we have] imagined.'[156]

To some readers all this may sound grandiose, but the point being made is a serious one. 'Love your life,'[157] Thoreau stated with disarming simplicity, and make no excuses. 'Every man is tasked to make his life, even in its details, worthy of the contemplation of his most elevated and critical hour.'[158] Thoreau thought that there are as many ways to live 'as there can be drawn radii from one centre,'[159] and he desired that there 'be as many different persons in the world as possible.'[160] But he also saw 'how easily and insensibly we fall into a particular route, and make a beaten track for ourselves,'[161] how easily we fall into the 'deep ruts of tradition and conformity.'[162] This troubled Thoreau deeply, for he thought that if we do not live our lives *deliberately*, if we only get out of bed because of 'the mechanical nudgings of some servitor,'[163] then we are just sleep-walking through life, injuring eternity by killing time. 'Little is to be expected of that day, if it can be called a day, to which we are not awakened by our Genius.'[164] Thoreau, to be sure, is speaking not so much to geniuses here, as to the genius (or poet) in us all. Take yourself and your life seriously, he is saying. Do not let yourself be swept along. Claim your freedom and exercise your capacity to create your own fate. Compose yourself! WAKE UP!

'Awakening' is one of the most prominent moral tropes in *Walden*. The epigraph to the book reads: 'I do not propose to write an ode to dejection, but to brag as lustily as chanticleer in the morning, standing on his roost, if only to wake my neighbors up.' And in the final paragraph of *Walden* we read: 'Only that day dawns to which we are awake. There is more day to dawn.'[165] This notion of 'awakening' brings us face to face with our focus question, which I hope has not been lost. If we are to know how much material wealth is *enough*, and thereby avoid labouring without end or purpose, then first we need to confront the question: 'Enough for *what*?' Put otherwise, we need to ask ourselves: 'What should we want material wealth *for*?' If we neglect this question, that is, if we neglect our 'proper pursuits,' we are at risk of wasting our lives in the pursuit of inessential trivialities and living lives of 'quiet desperation.' Thoreau was certainly not going to answer the question for us – we must each find our *'own* way'[166] in life, he properly insisted. But he did try to 'wake up his neighbors' who were asleep to the question. 'Moral reform,' he stated, 'is the effort to throw off sleep.... The millions are awake enough for physical labor; but only one in a million is awake enough for effective intellectual exertion, only one in a hundred millions to a poetic or divine life. To be awake is to be alive.'[167]

Thoreau began each day by getting up at dawn and bathing in the pond, which he claimed 'was a religious exercise, and one of the best things which I did.'[168] What could awaken us more immediately, what else could thrust us so intensely into a state of sensual excitement and awareness, than a plunge, first thing in the morning, into a clear, cold pond?[169] *Walden*, it could be said, seeks to do for its readers what bathing in the pond did for Thoreau. Should we never find time to read *Walden*, however, we might at least imagine Thoreau busting into our bedrooms at the break of dawn, as the first rays of sunlight are peeking over the Walden Woods, putting our sleepy selves over his shoulder and marching us toward the pond, then promptly throwing us in and afterward diving in himself. As we emerge from the chilling water, gasping for breath but now *fully awake*, we find ourselves face to face with Thoreau, who, with the sparkle of dawn in his eyes, puts his hands on our shoulders and says: *'Contact! Contact! Who* are we? *Where* are we?'[170]

As I have said, Thoreau does not try to answer these perennial human questions for us, but he does insist that we must face them head on when shaping our attitudes to money and material things. If we do not face them, Thoreau argued, we cannot possibly understand the meaning or purpose of 'Economy.' Ask yourself: What is money really *for*?

At this important juncture we see just how distant the methodology of alternative economics is to that of most mainstream economic theory. Economists typically assume that the 'ends' of consumer behaviour are arbitrary from an economic perspective, mere 'preferences,' and not a subject matter with which they need to concern themselves. The economist's job, rather, is to efficiently maximise the size of the economic pie, so that as many unquestioned 'preferences' as possible can be satisfied via free market transactions. Economists also tend to assume that human beings have an insatiable desire for material wealth, ownership, and consumption whose pursuit is limited only by scarcity of resources.[171] Thoreau's alternative economics rejects these assumptions. From his perspective, as we have seen, it makes no sense to pursue material wealth if the 'ends' of consumer behaviour are ignoble or childish, and thus the ends must be justified before the economic activity can be justified. The ends are inseparable from the means, such that we cannot judge individuals or societies to be 'successful' merely on the grounds that they are the richest, for they might spend all their money on trinkets, baubles, and other inane trivialities. As Thoreau asserted, 'The cart before the horse is neither beautiful nor useful.'[172] It follows that an alternative economist is necessarily concerned with the justifiability of 'preferences,' and does not just accept them as 'given.' Furthermore, Thoreau did not conceptualise human beings as economic agents who have insatiable desires for material wealth and who are always frustrated by scarcity of resources. Far from it, he thought that we can know when we have enough, if only we put our minds to the matter. True wealth, according to this view, is not so much about getting what we want as wanting what we have. And just perhaps this abundance is attainable by a simple act of will? Again, the words of Lao Tzu ring true: 'Those who know they have enough are rich.'[173]

5. COMFORTS, LUXURIES, AND TOOLS

The purpose of the preceding section was to show that we cannot answer the question, 'how much is *enough*?' until we have first answered the question, 'enough for *what*?' Having exposed that relationship, we are now in a position to return to our examination of what attitude Thoreau adopts in relation to material resources beyond the necessaries of life. On this question his alternative economics entails – at times implicitly, at times explicitly – a categorisation of material resources into comforts, luxuries, and tools. Discussing those three categories is the purpose of this section.

We all want the material resources needed to pursue our chief purpose in life, whatever that purpose might be. But might there be times when our pursuit of material resources does not support but actually interferes with our chief purpose? Everybody wants *enough*, but how much is *too much*? The answer to this question, once again, will be shaped by the answer given to, 'enough for *what*?' and there is no single right answer to that question. We will see, however, that Thoreau's alternative economics provides a framework for inquiry that each of us can apply to our own lives, despite the fact that we each have unique life goals. Our answers to the questions posed will probably be different, since our life goals will probably be different, but I contend that alternative economics at least gets us struggling with the right questions, which is no minor accomplishment.

To begin with, consider a scenario in which a person is comfortably able to secure the necessaries of life, but no more. Should this person spend their time despairing at how little they have? Or are the necessaries alone enough to live well and to be free? Although Thoreau does not advocate that we only seek the necessaries and no more – and never is it his intention to glorify true poverty – he does insist (as a self-respecting Stoic) that if it so happens that our fate is to live a life founded upon the necessaries only, this is no cause for despair, necessarily. In such circumstances, he argued, we may be simply 'confined to the most significant and vital experiences [and] compelled to deal with the material which yields the most sugar... It is life near the bone where it is sweetest.'[174] His point is that once our basic needs are met, 'Money is not required to buy one necessary of the soul,'[175] which is but an inflection of the old adage that, 'the best things in life are free.' With the necessaries of life secured, a strong-minded and cheerful Stoic might still be able to fall in love, experience the joys of conversation and friendship, saunter through Nature and delight in her 'inexhaustible entertainment,'[176] be part of a community or enjoy solitary contemplation, participate in political life, have aesthetic or spiritual experiences, meditate, sing, laugh, etc. – none of which need to rely on money, or much money. As Thoreau put it:

'The setting sun is reflected from the windows of the almshouse as brightly as from the rich man's abode; the snow melts before its door as early in the spring. I do not see but a quiet mind may live as contentedly there, and have as cheering thoughts, as in a palace.'[177] In this context I cannot resist also quoting John Burroughs:

> [T]o be in direct and personal contact with the sources of your material life; to find the universal elements enough; to find the air and the water exhilarating; to be refreshed by a morning walk or an evening saunter; to find a quest of wild berries more satisfying than a gift of tropical fruit; to be thrilled by the stars at night; to be elated over a bird's nest or a wild flower in spring – these are some of the rewards of the simple life.[178]

As noted, Thoreau had possessions that went beyond the bare necessaries of life, though a materially simple life he certainly lived. We know he built himself a small cabin with but one room, and ate a lot of beans. He tells us that his furniture, part of which he made himself, consisted of a bed, a table, a desk, three chairs, a looking-glass three inches in diameter, a pair of tongs and andirons, a kettle, a skillet, and a frying-pan, a dipper, a wash-bowl, two knives and forks, three plates, one cup, one spoon, a jug for oil, a jug for molasses, and a japanned lamp.[179] Though he did not wear rags, he happily wore patches on his old clothing, and since he spent so much time outdoors his clothing looked well-worn and weather-beaten. Beyond these things, he stated that a few implements, such as 'a knife, an axe, a spade, a wheelbarrow, etc., and for the studious, lamplight, stationery, and access to a few books, rank next to necessaries, and can all be obtained at a trifling cost.'[180] According to Thoreau, if our goals are 'higher' then we should recognise the limited need for money and possessions in our lives. '[M]y greatest skill has been to want but little,'[181] he insisted.

As mentioned above, in addition to the material resources that are simply indispensable to life – Food, Clothing, Shelter, and Fuel – Thoreau also has three other categories of material resources. 'Comforts,' which serve to make our lives more pleasurable; 'luxuries,' which are superfluous, even harmful; and 'tools,' which serve to further our self-development and help us achieve our life goals. A few words will suffice to clarify the place these latter three categories have in Thoreau's alternative economics.

With respect to comforts, let us begin by noting that Thoreau was far from being an ascetic or a puritan. He never denied himself material resources because he sought spiritual nourishment from deprivation. Nor did he disapprove of pleasure. Far from it, pleasure was very important to him. For this reason, he felt that there was a proper place for comforts in life, material things that were not necessary to life, but just made life better, happier, more pleasant. Nevertheless, Thoreau felt that we have to be careful. The risk with comforts is that they are addictive. They can easily become the chief focus in our lives, consuming a lot of our time and energy, and Thoreau felt that the purpose in life is not to be comfortable, but to live passionately. Furthermore, sometimes the time and money that we exchange for comforts can simply be a bad trade, in the sense that the comforts ultimately cost more in terms of 'life' than they come to. And so it is not that Thoreau is against the warmth of comforts, it is just that he thought we are easily cooked. When answering the question, 'how much is enough?', alternative economics requires that we keep these considerations in mind.

If Thoreau was guarded with respect to comforts, he was even more so with respect to luxuries. Perhaps there are some people, he claimed, who could build more magnificently and live more lavishly than the richest do now, 'without ever impoverishing themselves,'[182] but he had his doubts about whether any such people exist. Luxuries, he believed, were superfluous to a good life and, indeed, tended to cause more harm than good to those who were unlucky enough to be burdened by them. Referring to the superfluities of luxurious furniture and ornaments, he writes:

> At present our houses are cluttered and defiled with it, and a good housewife would sweep out the greater part into the dust hole, and not leave her morning's work undone. Morning work! By the blushes of Aurora and the music of Memnon, what should be man's *morning work* in this world? I had three pieces of limestone on my desk, but I was terrified to find that they required to be dusted daily, when the furniture of my mind was all undusted still, and threw them out the window in disgust.[183]

Thoreau's point here, as it has been so often before, is that we must not waste our limited time and attention on things that are irrelevant to our 'morning work,' that is, to our 'proper pursuits.' For it is not just that luxuries are superfluous to a good life – a criticism which sounds rather benign. More malignantly, they function to distract us from our proper pursuits, essentially wasting our time and thus our lives. In a famous phrase which we have already had occasion to consider, Thoreau claimed: 'Most of the luxuries, and many of the so-called comforts of life, are not only not indispensable, but positive hindrances to the elevation of mankind.'[184] And on this basis – again inverting mainstream economic perspectives – Thoreau provocatively stated: 'a man is rich in proportion to the number of things he can afford to let alone.'[185]

This is not the end of it, however. Although Thoreau was critical of having and consuming luxuries, he was also critical of those people – Thoreau would call them 'fools' – who feel greatly deprived, despite their comforts, because they are without luxuries: 'men have come to such a pass that they frequently starve, not for want of necessaries, but for want of luxuries.'[186] This point is important, though it is limited to the middle and upper classes, not the poor. If we read between the lines, Thoreau is suggesting that whatever dissatisfaction people have with their material situations may well be the result of failing to look properly at their lives, rather than the result of any genuine lack. Let us not be like the man who complained of 'hard times because he could not afford to buy him[self] a crown!'[187] That type of complaint is symptomatic of what some social critics are today calling 'affluenza,' understood as a collective psychological disorder that leaves people feeling deprived despite their plenty.[188]

On top of all this, Thoreau was simply unimpressed by and even pitiful of the luxuriously rich, 'that seemingly wealthy, but most terribly impoverished class of all, who have accumulated dross, but know not how to use it, or get rid of it, and thus have forged their own golden or silver fetters.'[189] When the 'degraded rich' start living decent lives, Thoreau spat in their direction, 'then perhaps I may look at your baubles and find them ornamental.'[190]

And finally, there are tools, those things which genuinely serve to further our self-development and help us achieve our life goals. If we look to Thoreau's own life, in the category of 'tools' he would have included books, stationary, a lamp, his flute, hand lenses, wheel-barrow, etc. What *we* include in this category depends on what our life goals are, but we should always bear in mind that tools may no longer help us, just as comforts may no longer bring pleasure, when used unwisely or excessively.[191] 'Men have become the tools of their tools,' Thoreau asserted.[192] 'The best works of art are the expression of man's struggle to free himself from this condition.'[193]

In essence, Thoreau's views on material resources could be expressed as follows. Throughout much of human history it was a constant struggle to secure the necessaries of life, and in such circumstances Thoreau perceived a certain wisdom and prudence in human decision-making, insofar as the guiding principle was to 'satisfy the more pressing wants first.'[194] But in affluent societies, where most have more than enough to live well, Thoreau would ask: 'are the more pressing wants satisfied now?'[195] The suggestion is that, unlike the wise and prudent primitive societies, we are satisfying less pressing wants (for superfluous comforts, luxuries, and tools) and neglecting what are for us more genuinely pressing wants, such as a flourishing inner life. That is only his general hypothesis, however. We must test it ourselves.

6. Appropriate Technology

What about technology? Must the simple liver indiscriminately renounce it? Thoreau thought that it is certainly better to accept than reject the advantages, though so dearly bought, which the invention and industry of humankind offer – provided, of course, that they are genuine advantages.[196] But he warned that often with these 'modern improvements' there is 'an illusion about them; there is not always a positive advance.... Our inventions are want to be pretty toys, which distract us from serious things. They are an improved means to an unimproved end.'[197] It is all very well to invent or be able to afford some new gadget, Thoreau was saying, but we should look upon new technologies with a measure of scepticism, for however ingenious and marvellous the invention may seem, it will likely have unintended side-effects and even shape who we are as persons, in ways that are not always obvious or positive. Looking to our own day, the television, for example, is a remarkable human achievement, and yet, aside from sleeping and working, the television now consumes more time of the typical North American or Briton than any other activity, and other 'advanced societies' watch almost as much.[198] One does not have to be an elitist to have doubts about whether this is really the best way to spend our freedom. The point is that if we do not know what to *do* with technology, then it can be life-debilitating rather than life-enhancing.

Trying to get us to question the purpose of various technologies and whether they actually improve our lives, Thoreau wrote:

> We are in great haste to construct a magnetic telegraph from Maine to Texas; but Maine and Texas, it may be, have nothing important to communicate.... As if the main object were to talk fast and not to talk sensibly. We are eager to tunnel under the Atlantic and bring the Old World some weeks nearer to the New; but perchance the first news that will leak through into the broad, flapping American ear will be that the Princess Adelaide has the whooping cough.[199]

The problem is that technology is often *just there* – fascinating, new, socially celebrated, affordable, and available – and it is so easy to fall into the trap of thinking that, since earlier generations did without it, we 'moderns'/'postmoderns' must therefore have progressed, that we are necessarily better off. Pernicious nonsense, Thoreau would say. We must show some discrimination in terms of what we choose to celebrate. If some new technology genuinely furthers our life goals and does not distract us from more important activities, then, by all means, we should take advantage of it. But Thoreau warned that all too often – in insidious ways – technology costs more than it comes to.

Two reasons that made Thoreau particularly suspicious of technology were (1) that we have to spend time working to earn money to afford technology, and he wonders whether we might regularly be better off without the technology and with more free time; and (2) that technology tends to distance us from the natural environment and can affect our life experiences for the worse. Both these points are masterfully illustrated in the following passage:

> One [friend] says to me, 'I wonder that you do not lay up money; you love to travel; you might take the cars and go to Fitchburg today and see the country.' But I am wiser than that. I have learned that the swiftest traveler is he that goes afoot. I say to my friend, Suppose we try who will get there first. The distance is thirty miles; the fare ninety cents. That is almost a day's wages. I remember when wages were sixty cents a day for laborers on this very road. Well, I start now on foot, and get there before night; I have travelled at that rate by the week together. You will in the meanwhile have earned your fare, and arrive there some time tomorrow, or possibly this evening, if you are lucky enough to get a job in season. Instead of going to Fitchburg, you will be working here the greater part of the day. And so, if the railroad reached round the world, I think that I should keep ahead of you; and as for seeing the country and getting experience of that kind, I should have to cut your acquaintance altogether. [200]

Travelling by train might seem to be the most 'efficient' way to travel, but Thoreau challenges us to rethink how this new technology affects our experience and what are its full costs, comprehensively defined. And although Thoreau's example here considers transportation only, the points he makes are generally applicable to all our decisions relating to technology.

To the objection that Thoreau is advocating an unsophisticated primitive existence, the appropriate response is twofold: first, that although he often damned technologies as debilitating luxuries, he did not deny that they could also be enabling tools worthy of praise and exploitation; secondly, Thoreau would have suggested that just perhaps there is a sophistication and elegance to the clothesline, the bicycle, and the water tank, that the dryer, the automobile, and the desalination plant, decidedly lack. Conversely, perhaps there is a certain primitiveness to technological gimmicks. As

Leonardo da Vinci once wrote: 'Simplicity is the ultimate sophistication.'

7. WORKING HOURS

Before closing this part of the discussion it may be worthwhile to reflect on Thoreau's attitude to working hours. His basic insight here, which is central to his alternative economics, can be expressed quite briefly, since it has been implicit throughout much of what has already been discussed and now just needs bringing to the surface.

We only have a limited amount of time on earth with which to live our lives, and out of self-respect we should not waste that time. Indeed, Thoreau suggested that we should be as covetous of our time as most people are of their money. On this subject he spoke not to those who are 'well employed, in whatever circumstances, and they know whether they are well employed or not.'[201] Rather, he directed his attention mainly to 'the mass of men who are discontented,'[202] those people who are not passionate about their working lives and who seek more time to do other, more inspiring things. Thoreau suggested that in affluent societies more time is probably available, if only one's material wants are reduced and controlled. Conversely, he warned that if one's material wants are allowed to creep up indefinitely, then one's working week will never decline and may even increase, despite considerable increases in wealth and advances in technology. This self-imposed labour of Sisyphus is one to which so many seem to have been condemned, but fortunately there is an alternative path to follow, a simpler way. Why not minimise and then stabilise one's material wants, and work less? In the same vein, instead of converting increases in income and productivity into more comforts and luxuries merely, as most do, why not convert those increases into more free time instead? It is well worth considering. Nevertheless, those who would not know what to do with more leisure if they were given it are bluntly advised by Thoreau 'to work twice as hard as they do now.'[203]

During his experiment, Thoreau discovered – and let this give us a moment's pause – that in living a life of voluntary simplicity he could meet all the expenses of living 'by working about six weeks in a year.'[204] This left him with the whole of his winters, as well as most of his summers, 'free and clear for study.'[205] Having thus secured his freedom, which is what he sought, he had no reason to envy (and indeed had reason to pity) the 'successful' capitalists, merchants, shopkeepers, mechanics, farmers, lawyers, doctors, etc. who were money rich but time poor. In one of his more acidic moments Thoreau even commented that those who spent their time earning superfluous money 'deserve[d] some credit for not having all committed suicide long ago.'[206] Their highest duty in life to accumulate money! Does any divinity stir within them?, Thoreau wondered. What are their destinies worth to them compared with money?[207]

Thoreau's central insight on the subject of working hours is powerfully captured in the following passage:

> Those slight labors which afford me a livelihood, and by which it is allowed that I am to some extent serviceable to my contemporaries, are as yet commonly a pleasure to me, and I am not often reminded that they are a necessity. So far I am successful. But I foresee that if my wants should be much increased, the labor required to supply them would become a drudgery. If I should sell both my forenoons and afternoons to society, as most appear to do, I am sure that for me there would be nothing worth left living for.... I wish to suggest that a man may be very industrious, and yet not spend his time well. There is no more fatal blunderer than he who consumes the greater part of his life getting a living.[208]

Thoreau saw his neighbours spending the best part of their lives accumulating dross in order to enjoy a questionable liberty in their final years. This reminded him of 'the Englishman who went to India to make a fortune first, in order that he might return to England and live the life of a poet. He should have gone up garret at once.'[209] Thoreau again returns to the metaphor of 'sleeping away life' to hammer home his point:

> I confess that I am astonished at the power of endurance, to say nothing of the moral insensibility, of my neighbors who confine themselves to shops and offices the whole day for weeks and months, aye, and years almost together. I know not what manner of stuff they are of, sitting there now at three o'clock in the afternoon, as if it were three o'clock in the morning.[210]

The fact that Thoreau was able to provide for his basic needs by working only six weeks per year, or thereabouts, should provoke those of us who work approximately 48 or 50 weeks a year, in jobs we do not always like, to at least reassess what exactly we are getting back for the time we are giving up. Even if we suppose that Thoreau's working hours were to some degree distorted for one reason or another, his arguments still deserve reflection. From the perspective of alternative economics, are we doing 'good business' by always trading our time for a higher material standard of living? Are we forced by the curse of labour to work so much? Or are we freer than we think we are?

Thoreau's view on the matter is perfectly clear: 'I am convinced, both by faith and experience, that to maintain one's self on this earth is not a hardship but a pastime, if we will live simply and wisely.'[211] This is perhaps the most important lesson that he learned while living in the woods, and it was a lesson that stayed with him for the rest of his life.

8. AFTER WALDEN

On 6 September 1847, Thoreau left his cabin at Walden Pond and again took up residence in Concord, where he remained for the rest of his years, a 'sojourner in civilized life.'[212] Though he always lived a life of voluntary simplicity, he came to accept that industrial capitalism was an impersonally dictated social order within which he had to live, however much he despised it.[213] Since his material needs were so few, however, for a long time he found that he barely had to work one month each spring and fall to support himself. Emerson once made a fairly representative list of some of Thoreau's various roles during these post-Walden years, a list which included 'building a boat or a fence, planting, grafting, surveying,' with 'short work' preferred to 'long engagements.'[214] Thoreau eventually settled on the trade of surveying, an occupation that allowed him to spend his time outside, wandering the countryside around Concord, which suited him ideally. These 'slight labors,' as we have just seen, were 'commonly a pleasure' to him, and he was 'not often reminded they [were] a necessity.'[215] Though surveying was not highly paid, it paid enough for him to generally work mornings only, leaving him with the afternoons and evenings absolutely free for his 'proper pursuits.' At the beginning of life, as at the end, Thoreau was very careful not to be seduced into exchanging his precious time for an insufficient amount of comforts and luxuries.

By the time he died in 1862, Thoreau had attained a certain recognised position as a writer, although the amount of money he earned from his writing and lecturing over his entire life was minute. But the fact that his books, essays, and poems barely sold was of little consequence. He had woven a kind of basket of a delicate texture, and although he had not made it worth anyone's while to buy them, he felt that it had nonetheless been worth his while to weave them.

8.1. *Was Thoreau's Experiment a Success?*

Even though Thoreau is now recognised as one of America's finest writers, the focus of our current study has been the alternative economics that he practiced during his experiment at Walden Pond, and the question that remains is: Was his experiment a success?

The question is a complex one, although perhaps not so complex as it is sometimes made out to be. If, in his experiment at the pond, we attribute to Thoreau the aim of living a life of complete independence and self-sufficiency – like Adam, or Robinson Crusoe, perhaps – a life in which he ate only what he grew and grew only what he ate, neither worked for another nor hired another, and avoided all trade and barter, then we must conclude that his experiment was a failure. Thoreau, after all, lived on Emerson's land; he borrowed an axe and other tools to get himself started; he set himself up in an unproductive corner of Massachusetts as a marginal commercial farmer whose cash crop did not bring in enough money to satisfy all his needs; he therefore hired himself out as a day labourer when he needed to make ends meet, and occasionally hired labour himself; [216] furthermore, he was no stranger in the village, and would sometimes dine comfortably with his family or at the Emerson residence. These are the types of reasons that led critics like James Russel Lowell to allege that '[Thoreau's] shanty life was a mere impossibility, so far as his own conception of it goes, as an entire independency of mankind.' [217]

But this is to misunderstand the nature of Thoreau's project, and to misjudge it on that account. There is nothing to indicate that Thoreau sought 'an entire independency of mankind.' He did not set out to reject features of civilisation that were of genuine advantage or to live as a hermit. Let us not forget that he lived a mile from society, *but only a mile*. My point, here, is that before we are in a position to judge the success of Thoreau's experiment we must have a proper understanding of its nature, and to help us understand this we should look to Thoreau's own carefully crafted words: 'My purpose in going to Walden Pond was neither to live cheaply nor live dearly there, but to transact some private business with the fewest obstacles.' [218] In one sense, as noted earlier, this 'private business' was simply to write in privacy. Since we now know that while he was at the pond he wrote *A Week on the Concord and Merrimack Rivers*, the bulk of *Walden*, and perhaps a draft of his essay 'Civil Disobedience' – three texts (especially the latter two) which are now considered among the greatest works of American literature – it would seem that his experiment at the pond must be judged a resounding success. But this is to move too quickly, perhaps, since earlier we saw that his 'private business' also included his struggle with the economic problem of how to live poetically in a world of scarce resources. To what extent can we say that this struggle was a success?

We have seen that to 'live poetically,' in Thoreau's sense, essentially involves: (1) providing for one's material needs in a way that is meaningful, fulfilling, and respectful of nature; and (2) having the freedom and independence for one's 'proper pursuits,' whatever they may be. On this basis, it would seem equally clear that, in his struggle for a poetic existence, Thoreau met with some real success in his experiment (even though it turned out that the struggle did not so much lead to a destination as much as it was an ongoing creative process). In hewing timber for his cabin on 'pleasant spring days, in which the winter of man's discontent was thawing'[219] he discovered 'the pleasure of construction,' he sang as he worked, and 'made no haste in [his] work, but rather made the of most it.'[220] He also tells us that, '[i]n those days, when my hands were much employed, I read but little, but the least scraps of paper which lay on the ground, my holder, or tablecloth, afforded me as much entertainment, in fact answered the same purpose as the Iliad.'[221] As for his work in the bean field, he tells of how hoeing his rows 'yielded an instant and immeasurable crop,'[222] and attached him to the earth in a way that was nourishing. Even when Thoreau felt the need to hire himself out as a labourer – an occupation which he deemed 'the most independent of any'[223] – it was not always time wasted. In one journal entry he wrote: 'Great thoughts hallow any labor. Today I earned seventy-five cents heaving manure out of a pen, and made a good bargain of it.'[224] Perhaps the most significant feature of his time at the pond, however, was his discovery that by living simply and generally relying on himself for his needs, he could maintain himself by working about six weeks per year only, leaving him with the whole of his winters, as well as most of his summers, 'free and clear for study,'[225] or, more generally, for following the bent of his genius.[226] On top of these successes, there are good reasons for thinking that throughout his time at the pond Thoreau was, quite simply, happy. 'My life was ecstasy,'[227] he wrote in the most successful expression of this feeling.

Nevertheless, before we can conclude that Thoreau's experiment at the pond was largely a success, we must confront the question: 'Why, then, did he leave?' After all, he only stayed for two years and two months, after which time he returned to live in Concord. But if he had secured the freedom, tranquillity, and happiness that he sought, why did he not remain at the pond his whole life? This is sometimes considered a fatal blow, proof that his experiment was an idealised distortion of social and economic reality, one that not even Thoreau could sustain.[228] I think we must hesitate, however, before judging his experiment a failure on this account. During his time at the pond Thoreau had learned by experience that very little is actually needed to live well and to be free, if only life is approached with the right attitude. Furthermore, he had cultivated a deep understanding of 'the essential facts of life' and developed a genuine love of simplicity. All this meant that he was able to live with an 'inexpressible confidence'[229] and 'calm trust in the future,'[230] knowing that if he were ever to lose all his possessions he would be 'nearly as well off as before.'[231] Could he not then leave his experiment behind yet take its lessons with him? Was he not correct in his claim that, '[i]t is not the tub that makes Diogenes, the Jove-born, but Diogenes the tub'?[232] We should not dismiss in advance the possibility that those who successfully prosecute an inward voyage might learn to live in acquisitive society and yet above it, liberated from imprisonment within its values.[233]

'I left the woods for as good a reason as I went there,' Thoreau tells us near the end of *Walden*. 'Perhaps it seemed to me that I had several more lives to live, and could not spare any more for that one.'[234] It should not surprise us that there is a measure of uncertainty in this explanation, given that his time at the pond was an enormously positive and creative period in his life. It would surely have been very tempting to stay. Indeed, a journal entry written five years after leaving the pond reads: 'But why I changed—? Why I left the woods? I do not think I can tell. I have often wished myself back.'[235] In another entry, however, he was less regretful: 'Perhaps I wanted a change.... Perhaps if I lived there much longer I might live there forever – One would think twice before he accepted heaven on such terms.'[236] This last point, I think, gets to the heart of the matter. Sublime though his experience was at the pond, Thoreau's ethic of self-cultivation and his constant yearning for self-renewal required a stance of openness to new and diverse experiences. Expressing this need to move onward and upward, he wrote: 'I did not wish to take a cabin passage, but rather to go before the mast and on the deck of the world, for there I could best see the moonlight amid the mountains. I do not wish to go below now.'[237]

45

In the end, whether *we* judge Thoreau's experiment to be a success or a failure is arguably beside the point, since Thoreau cared little for the 'smoke of opinion'[238] and instead chose to think for himself. His own assessment of his time at the pond is perhaps best represented in the following passage:

> I learned this, at least, by my experiment: that if one advances confidently in the direction of his dreams, and endeavors to live the life which he has imagined, he will meet with a success unexpected in common hours. He will put some things behind, will pass an invisible boundary; new, universal, and more liberal laws will begin to establish themselves around and within him; or the old laws be expanded, and interpreted in his favor in a more liberal sense, and he will live with the license of a higher order of beings. In proportion as he simplifies his life, the laws of the universe will appear less complex, and solitude will not be solitude, nor poverty poverty, nor weakness weakness. If you have built castles in the air, your work need not be lost; that is where they should be. Now put the foundations under them.[239]

9. CONCLUSION

So ends our examination of Thoreau's living experiment at Walden Pond and the alternative economics that he developed there. Or does this examination, by its very nature, have no end? After all, living a life of 'simplicity, independence, magnanimity, and trust,' involves solving 'some of the problems of life, not only theoretically, but practically also.'[240] And this is not so much a destination as it is an ongoing creative process. Our study has left much unsaid, necessarily, and perhaps the discussion has raised more questions than it has answered. But perhaps that is how Thoreau would have wanted it. He was not interested in giving us detailed instructions on how to live a simpler life; nor did he want to save us the trouble of thinking for ourselves. Rather, he wanted to stoke the fire in our souls and inspire us with ideals. 'Don't spend your time in drilling soldiers,' he once wrote, 'who may turn out hirelings after all, but give to the undrilled peasantry a *country* to fight for.'[241]

Ever since he was a young man, Thoreau believed that the object of life was 'something else than acquiring property'[242] and that true success did not consist in 'much money, many houses' but in 'trying to better [our] condition in a higher sense than this.'[243] He had no desire to succeed in the desperate measure of getting rich or comfortable merely. He felt that there was a very different ideal to fight for: to weave one's trade with the Celestial Empire into one's everyday affairs – that is, to live poetically. By striving with almost unrivalled determination to live in this spirit, Thoreau was able to compose as an aesthetic project the meaning of his own life, 'to invent and get a patent for himself.'[244] A couplet that he scribbled down in his journal truthfully describes his greatest achievement:

My life has been the poem I would have writ,
But I could not both live and utter it.

Thoreau's life is a reminder that dedicated individuals can establish a simpler, freer way of life for themselves, simply by adopting a new frame of mind and acting upon it with creativity and conviction. Doing so may not be easy, of course, since it will involve moving in the opposite direction to where most of humankind is marching. But as Thoreau would say: 'If a man does not keep pace with his companions, perhaps it is because he hears a different drummer. Let him step to the music which he hears, however measured or far away.'[245] Thoreau would also advise us not to wait for our politicians or peers to attain enlightenment before we begin our journey toward simplicity, for it might be a long time before they wake up. Those who have the courage to go forward alone, however, can start today.[246]

As we are propelled into the 21st century by the forces of a materialistic history, the reasons for returning to – or rather, advancing toward – Thoreau are compelling. To put it proverbially, if we do not change direction, we are likely to end up where we are going. Our planet's ecosystems urgently need us to explore alternative ways to live, and one promising way to lessen our impact on nature is to reject the materialistic lifestyles of consumer culture and voluntarily embrace 'a simpler life' of reduced consumption. Furthermore, in a world where extreme poverty exists amidst such plenty, there are powerful humanitarian arguments in favour of taking less so that others can have more. As Mahatma Gandhi once said: 'Live simply so that others may simply live.'[247] But a life of voluntary simplicity need not generate any sense of deprivation. Indeed, the Voluntary Simplicity Movement is demonstrating through the lives of millions of participants that by lowering our 'standard of living' (measured by income or consumption) we can actually increase our 'quality of life' (measured by subjective wellbeing). Paradoxical though it may sound, voluntary simplicity is about living more with less. And perhaps this paradox has something to say to everyone, especially those of us who are every day bombarded with thousands of cultural and institutional messages insisting that 'more is always better.' Voluntary simplicity is an art of living that is aglow with the insight that 'just enough is plenty.'

ENDNOTES

[1] Henry David Thoreau, 'Walden' in Carl Bode (ed.), *The Portable Thoreau* (1982).

[2] Ralph Waldo Emerson, 'The American Scholar' in Carl Bode (ed.), *The Portable Emerson* (1981) 68.

[3] Thoreau once said, 'The fact is that I am a mystic, a transcendentalist, and a natural philosopher to boot.' Bob Blaisdell (ed.), *Thoreau: A Book of Quotations* (2000) 11. For an excellent examination of Thoreau's spirituality, see Alan D. Hodder, *Thoreau's Ecstatic Witness* (2001).

[4] Henry David Thoreau, 'Civil Disobedience' in Carl Bode (ed.), *The Portable Thoreau* (1982) 109.

[5] In reviewing Thoreau's history of employment, I am indebted to the more detailed account given in Carl Bode (ed.), *The Portable Thoreau* (1982) 1–27.

[6] In any case, as he was later to admit, 'As I did not teach for the good of my fellow-men, but simply for a livelihood, this was a failure.' Thoreau, above n 1, 323.

[7] Carl Bode (ed.), *The Portable Thoreau* (1982) 15.

[8] See Fred Lorch, 'Thoreau and the Organic Principle in Poetry' (1938) LIII *PMLA* 286.

[9] H. Daniel Peck (ed.), *A Year in Thoreau's Journal: 1851* (1993) 21.

[10] Ibid.

[11] Thoreau, above n 1, 306.

[12] Ibid.

[13] Ibid (emphasis in original).

[14] Henry David Thoreau, 'Life without Principle' in Carl Bode (ed.), *The Portable Thoreau* (1982) 632.

[15] Ibid.

[16] Ibid 650.

[17] Ibid 632.

[18] Ibid.

[19] Ibid 634.

[20] Thoreau, above n 1, 262.

[21] Thoreau, above n 14, 634.

[22] Ibid 640.

[23] Ibid 634.

[24] Ibid 636.

[25] Thoreau, above n 1, 261.

[26] Ibid 260.
[27] Ibid.
[28] See Goldian Vanenbroeck (ed.), *Less is More: The Art of Voluntary Poverty* (1991) 116.
[29] Thoreau, above n 1, 286.
[30] Ibid 261.
[31] Ibid.
[32] Ibid.
[33] Ibid 568.
[34] Ibid 269.
[35] Ibid 263.
[36] I am indebted to Carl Bode for this reference. See Carl Bode (ed.), *The Portable Thoreau* (1982) 25.
[37] Ibid.
[38] William Wordsworth, 'The World is Too Much With Us; Late and Soon' in John Hayden (ed.), *William Wordsworth: Selected Poems* (1994) 166.
[39] Thoreau, above n 1, 308.
[40] Ibid 312.
[41] Ibid.
[42] Ibid 345.
[43] Ibid 345–6.
[44] Ibid 337.
[45] Ibid 266.
[46] Ibid.
[47] Ibid 264–5.
[48] Ibid 274.
[49] Ibid 264.
[50] Samuel Alexander (ed.), *Voluntary Simplicity: The Poetic Alternative to Consumer Culture* (2009).
[51] Thoreau, above n 1, 343.
[52] Ibid.
[53] Ibid 343–4.
[54] Ibid 275.
[55] One of Thoreau's motivations for going to Walden Pond was to write, 'A Week on the Concord and Merrimack Rivers,' which he did. See Carl Bode (ed.), *The Portable Thoreau* (1982) 138–227.
[56] Thoreau, above n 1, 267.
[57] Ibid 275.
[58] Ibid 344.
[59] Ibid 344.
[60] Ibid 344.

[61] Henry David Thoreau, 'The Service,' quoted in Leo Stoller, *After Walden* (1957) 16.

[62] Thoreau, above n 1, 273.

[63] See Leo Stoller, *After Walden* (1957) 6–7. Stoller suggests that if Thoreau's poems and essays had brought him money, the Walden Experiment may never have eventuated.

[64] Thoreau, above n 1, 274.

[65] Ibid 324.

[66] Ibid 275.

[67] It was Thomas Carlyle who once said, 'The Fraction of Life can be increased in value not so much by increasing your Numerator as by lessening your Denominator.' See Thomas Carlyle, *Sartor Resartus* (1999) 145.

[68] Thoreau, above n 1, 272.

[69] Ibid.

[70] See generally, Richard A. Posner, *The Economics of Justice* (1981).

[71] Thoreau, above n 1, 275.

[72] Ibid 276.

[73] Judith Saunders, 'Transcendental Capitalist at Walden,' in Harold Bloom (ed.), *Henry David Thoreau's "Walden"* (1987) 59.

[74] Henry David Thoreau, '*Walden*' in Carl Bode (ed.), *The Portable Thoreau* (1982) 363.

[75] Ibid 364.

[76] Ibid 364.

[77] Henry David Thoreau, *Journal* (1962) 185.

[78] Thoreau, above n 1, 296.

[79] Ibid 400, 457.

[80] Ibid 483.

[81] Stanley Cavell, *The Senses of Walden: An Expanded Edition*, 1981) 88–9.

[82] Saunders, above n 73, 59–60.

[83] Thoreau, above n 1, 440.

[84] Ibid 286.

[85] Saunders, above n 73.

[86] Thoreau, above n 1, 324.

[87] I have been assisted in the following discussion by these texts: Stanley Cavell, *The Senses of Walden: An Expanded Edition* (1981); Philip Cafaro, *Thoreau's Living Ethics: "Walden" and the Pursuit of Virtue* (2004); Leo Stoller, *After Walden* (1957); Leonard Neufeldt, *The Economist: Henry Thoreau and Enterprise* (1989); Harold Bloom (ed.),

Henry David Thoreau's "Walden" (1987); Christian Becker, 'Thoreau's Economic Philosophy' (2008) 15(2) *European Journal of the History of Economic Thought* 211; Thomas D. Birch and Fred Metting, 'The Economic Design of Walden' (1992) 65(4) *The New England Quarterly* 587; Richard Prud'Homme, '*Walden's* Economy of Living' (2001) 20(3) *Raritan* 107.

[88] Thoreau, above n 1, 267–8.

[89] I should make clear that Thoreau is not suggesting that there is necessarily a conflict or trade-off here between such things as 'developing higher capacities' and 'obtaining the necessaries of life.' As we have seen and will see again, his aim is to ensure that there is no conflict here; that is, he seeks to develop his higher capacities *as* he provides for himself. But, as a matter of basic instinct, Thoreau is pointing out that should a conflict actually arise, then securing necessaries of life will always be prioritised over higher development. That is, when starving, one will look for food before reading Shakespeare or watching the sunset.

[90] Thoreau, above n 1, 267

[91] Ibid 267.

[92] Ibid 280.

[93] Ibid 281.

[94] Ibid 281.

[95] Ibid 282.

[96] Ibid 280.

[97] Ibid 276.

[98] Ibid 278.

[99] Ibid.

[100] Ibid 279.

[101] Ibid.

[102] Ibid 277.

[103] Ibid.

[104] Ibid 278.

[105] Ibid 282.

[106] Ibid 283.

[107] Ibid 283–285.

[108] Ibid 284.

[109] Ibid 284.

[110] Ibid 286.

[111] Ibid 288. I am reminded here of the following passage from John Ruskin: 'Lately in the wreck of a Californian ship, one of the passengers fastened a belt about him with two hundred pounds of gold in it, with which he was found afterwards at the bottom. Now, as he was sinking –

had he the gold? Of had the gold him?' See Goldian Vanenbroeck (ed.), *Less is More: The Art of Voluntary Poverty* (1991) 41.

[112] Thoreau, above n 1, 289 (emphasis in original).

[113] Ibid 304.

[114] Ibid 290.

[115] Ibid 300.

[116] Ibid.

[117] Ibid 300–1.

[118] Ibid 301.

[119] Ibid 288.

[120] Ibid 304.

[121] Ibid 295.

[122] Ibid 304.

[123] Ibid 315.

[124] Ibid 309–10.

[125] These expenses included seeds, rice, Indian meal and salt to make his own bread, oil for his lamp, etc.

[126] Thoreau, above n 1, 310.

[127] Ibid.

[128] Ibid 284.

[129] Ibid 404–5.

[130] Nathaniel Hawthorne, *Mosses from an Old Manse* (New edn, 1857).

[131] Thoreau, above n 1, 406.

[132] Ibid 406.

[133] Cafaro, above n 87, 98.

[134] Thoreau, above n 1, 408.

[135] Ibid 408.

[136] Henry David Thoreau, 'Walking' in Carl Bode (ed.), *The Portable Thoreau* (1982) 592.

[137] Thoreau, above n 1, 518.

[138] Thoreau, above n 1, 409.

[139] Cafaro, above n 87, 99. Thoreau's point is not that factory and office work are not valuable. His suggestion is that the drive to maximise profits is disconnecting more and more people from the simple pleasures of contact with nature in their working lives. Thoreau is questioning whether the increased profits that arise from factory and office work is worth that disconnection from nature.

[140] Thoreau, above n 1, 266. Thoreau also quotes Confucius: 'To know that we know what we know, and that we do not know what we do not know, that is true knowledge.' Thoreau, above n 1, 267.

---

[141] Ibid 319.

[142] Ibid 309.

[143] Ibid 268.

[144] Ibid 269.

[145] Ibid 270–1.

[146] Ibid 267–8.

[147] Ibid 261.

[148] Ibid 271.

[149] See Philip Cafaro, 'Less is More' in Samuel Alexander (ed.), *Voluntary Simplicity: The Poetic Alternative to Consumer Culture* (2009)127–134 (applying and discussing this calculus in the context of food consumption).

[150] Thoreau, above n 1, 260. See also, Cafaro, above n 87, 80.

[151] Friedrich Nietzsche, *The Gay Science* (2001) Section 299. See also, Alexander Nehamas, *Nietzsche: Life as Literature* (1985).

[152] In many places Thoreau talks of poetry with respect to life, rather than verse. For example, in 'Life without Principle,' he writes: 'The poet... must sustain his body by his poetry.' Thoreau, above n 14, 636. See also, Thoreau, above n 1, at 300 and 308. Stoller cites several other examples from Thoreau's *Journals*. See Stoller, above n 87, at 106, 114, 116, 119, 121. See also, Lorch, above n 8.

[153] Percy Bysshe Shelly, *A Defence of Poetry* (2007 [1840]) 12.

[154] On this point, see Michel Foucault, 'On the Geneaology of Ethics,' in Paul Rabinove, *Ethics* (2000) 261–2: '[I]n our society, art has become something that is related only to objects and not to individuals or to life. That art is something which is specialized or done by experts. But couldn't everyone's life become a work of art? Why should the lamp or the house be an art object but not our life? ... From the idea that the self is not given to us, I think that there is only one practical consequence: we have to create ourselves as a work of art.'

[155] Thoreau, above n 1, 343.

[156] Ibid 562.

[157] Ibid 560.

[158] Ibid 343.

[159] Ibid 266.

[160] Ibid 325.

[161] Ibid 562.

[162] Ibid 562.

[163] Ibid 342.

[164] Ibid 342.

[165] Ibid 572.

[166] Ibid 325.

[167] Ibid 343.

[168] Ibid 341.

[169] See Cafaro, above n 87, 19–21.

[170] Henry David Thoreau, *The Maine Woods*, edited by Joseph Moldenhaur (1974) 71.

[171] Cafaro, above n 87, 81.

[172] Thoreau, above n 1, 293.

[173] Above n 28.

[174] Thoreau, above n 1, 567.

[175] Ibid 568.

[176] Ibid 409.

[177] Ibid 566–7.

[178] Quoted in Clara Barrus, *Our Friend John Burroughs* (2008) 133.

[179] Thoreau, above n 1, 319.

[180] Ibid 269.

[181] Ibid 324.

[182] Ibid 271.

[183] Ibid 291.

[184] Ibid 269.

[185] Ibid 335.

[186] Ibid 316.

[187] Ibid 290.

[188] Clive Hamilton and Richard Denniss, *Affluenza: When Too Much is Never Enough* (2005); John De Graaf et al, *Affluenza: The All-Consuming Epidemic* (2nd edn, 2005); Oliver James, *Affluenza: How to be Successful and Stay Sane* (2007).

[189] Thoreau, above n 1, 271.

[190] Ibid 293.

[191] See Cafaro, above n 87, 84.

[192] Thoreau, above n 1, 292.

[193] Ibid.

[194] Ibid 294.

[195] Ibid.

[196] Ibid 295.

[197] Ibid 306.

[198] Richard Layard, *Happiness: Lessons from a New Science* (2005) 86.

[199] Thoreau, above n 1, 307.

[200] Ibid 307.

[201] Ibid 271.

[202] Ibid.

[203] Ibid 324.
[204] Ibid 323.
[205] Ibid 323.
[206] Thoreau, above n 136, 595.
[207] Ibid 263.
[208] Thoreau, above n 14, 636.
[209] Thoreau, above n 1, 308.
[210] Thoreau, above n 136, 595.
[211] Thoreau, above n 1, 325.
[212] Ibid 258.
[213] Stoller, above 87, 71.
[214] Ibid 52-3.
[215] Thoreau, above n 14, 636.
[216] See Stoller, above n 87, 31.
[217] Henry Stephens Salt et al, *Life of Henry David Thoreau* (1993) 51.
[218] Thoreau, above n 1, 275.
[219] Ibid 296.
[220] Ibid 297.
[221] Ibid 300.
[222] Ibid 408.
[223] Ibid 324.
[224] See Bode, above n 5, 15
[225] Thoreau, above n 1, 323.
[226] Ibid 310.
[227] 'In youth… I can remember that I was all alive, and inhabited my body with inexpressible satisfaction; both its weariness and its refreshment were sweet to me. This earth was the most glorious musical instrument, and I was audience to its strains,' as quoted from Thoreau's journals. See Stoller, above n 87, 69.
[228] Stoller variously calls the experiment 'ineffectual,' 'unsuccessful,' and 'failed.' See Stoller, above n 87, at 3, 27, 108.
[229] Thoreau, above n 1, 410.
[230] Ibid.
[231] Ibid 310.
[232] From Thoreau's journals, as quoted in Stoller, above n 87, 112.
[233] See Stoller, above n 87, 49.
[234] Thoreau, above n 1, 562.
[235] David Robinson, *Natural Life: Thoreau's Worldly Transcendentalism* (2004) 79.
[236] Ibid.
[237] Thoreau, above n 1, 562.
[238] Ibid 264.

[239] Ibid 562.

[240] Ibid 270.

[241] From Thoreau's Journals, as quoted in Stoller, above n 87, 123.

[242] From Thoreau's Journals, as quoted in Stoller, above 87, 120

[243] Ibid.

[244] From Thoreau's Journals, as quoted in Stoller, above n 87, 108.

[245] Thoreau, above n 1, 564–5.

[246] Ibid 326.

[247] On Gandhi's view of simplicity see, Mahatma Gandhi, 'The Quest for Simplicity: My Idea of Swaraj,' in Majid Rahnema (ed.) *The Post-Development Reader* (1997) 306–7.

CPSIA information can be obtained
at www.ICGtesting.com
Printed in the USA
LVOW08s0736160117
520988LV00019B/427/P